THE
D⬤NUT
COOKBOOK

Zihon Press

THE DONUT COOKBOOK

A Baked Donut Recipe Book with Easy and Delicious Donuts
that Your Family and Kids Will Love

MAVIS BENNETT

Table of Contents

DISCLAIMER

The information provided in this book is for educational purposes only. If you have any health issues or pre-existing conditions, please consult your doctor before using the recipes. Cooking results may vary from individual to individual. All users should note that the book is for informational purposes only and the author or publisher does not accept any responsibilities for any liabilities or damages, directly or indirectly, resulting from the use of this book.

1

YUMMY AND IRRESTIBLE DONUTS!

Who could ever resist a tempting donut? Hardly anyone! Most people will start to drool just by looking at a delicious donut. Indeed, donuts are a popular snack or dessert in many countries around the globe. Whether you have a sweet tooth or not, there is a perfect donut in this book that you'll surely love. It's always fun to have delicious and irresistible donuts!

A Blissful Donut Variety

Yes, it is true! Donuts come in various shapes, flavors, texture and basically wherever your imagination goes. Donuts can be molded to form rings, balls, buns, sticks, twisted, square, bars, something muffin-like, and many other imaginable shapes. Some are fruity, while some are meaty and some are just plain. Additionally, donuts are sometimes coated, stuffed, glazed, frosted, sprinkled, filled, topped, fried, or baked.

Most donut varieties are divided into mainly cake and raised types. Donuts that rise are added with yeast as leavening agent. These will need to rise before cooking, which results in lighter and more airy donuts. Cream-filled and jelly donuts belong to this group. Cake donuts on the other hand, rely on baking powder or soda as leavening. Traditionally, these will need to be chilled overnight prior to rolling for an easier handling but it can also be baked right away. The cake donut batter usually results in a denser than yeasted donut and just as the name suggests, these types usually have a cake-like taste or texture. For sure, fried donuts are the most commonly sold commercially, but are often very unhealthy. This makes the baked donuts a clear winner whenever you are making your own donuts. Baked donuts usually have better textures and they give a palatable aroma that also makes then even more delightful and sumptuous. Better yet, baked donuts are healthier and carry fewer calories and not too much oil. I like to put it this way: Bake More—Less Guilt! So try baking your donuts, it's a "hole" lot of fun!

Furthermore, to make things even more exciting, this donut recipe book is loaded with a wholesome variety of delicious baked donuts for every occasion. You and your family will surely love these sumptuous donuts.

QUICK DONUT BAKING TIPS

Here are some tips and techniques for efficient donut baking:
Gather your dry ingredients ahead of time. Preparing all of it
early or even the night before helps well, and remember that
the leavening agents in baking powder are not activated until added
with the liquid.

- Proper measuring is very important to successful donut baking. Weighing is more precise and consistent than measuring. It also minimizes bowls and utensils used. But if you prefer to measure use the scoop-and-scrape method in measuring dry ingredients. For more accurate results, scoop the cup into the ingredient and sweep a knife across; do not pat nor tamp down the ingredients in the cup.
- Greasing and flouring pans can be done in advance. Keep the greased pans in the fridge until you're ready to add the donut mixture.
- In combining the mixtures of wet and dry ingredients, NEVER over mix it. Stop when there are no more lumps or unmixed flour. Over mixed batter will give a tough and dry result.
- Using ingredients at the proper temperature is crucial in making sure they are well-incorporated. Butter, with few exceptions, is usually used at room temperature. Though this can vary depending on the season and how cold or warm your kitchen is. Same goes with eggs. Whether you will use them separated or not, they beat up much better at room temperature.
- When beating ingredients such as milk and eggs or egg yolks, first whisk the eggs or egg yolks to emulsify. This will ease the blending of other ingredients and eliminate "yolk burn".

- When using sticky ingredients such as honey, molasses, or corn syrup, spray the inside of your measuring cup with a non-stick cooking spray for a quicker pouting and cleaning.
- In pouring the batter into the pan, use a piping bag for a cleaner and balanced result. You may also use a pastry bag with one corner cut off or a ketchup bottle. Using a scoop for mini donuts also does the trick, depending on the consistency of your dough.

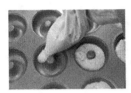

- Make sure to know the accuracy of your oven's temperature. Temperature control plays a crucial role in time management, product consistency, dough texture, flavor characteristics and shelf life. A range in temperature from 200°F to 205°F at the center of a lean dough is the largely accepted standard. This is the temperature essential for the structure throughout the final product to be adequately firm. For richer dough, the standard is 180°F to 190°F. A too low oven temperature causes the dough to expand to the fullest size before it gets the opportunity to set. The dough will then collapse and turn into a flat, dense mass. On the other hand, a too hot oven will cause the protein and starch in the outer layers to set too quickly, thus preventing further expansion.
- Size also matters. Small pieces of dough must be baked quickly in a hot oven so that the crust can fully form and brown without the crumb becoming too dry. On the other hand, large pieces must be baked slowly in a cooler oven so that the crust doesn't become overly thick and dark before the center of the crumb is perfectly cooked.
- In glazing, warm the glaze, not thin it. And coat donuts while warm. You may dip the donut in, drizzle it over, or place it in and bathe it with the glaze. Then immediately add the toppings while glaze or coating is still wet. It can be done by sprinkling, brushing, dipping, or sifting, depending on the texture of your toppings.
- It's necessary to let the baked donuts cool for a few minutes

in the pan before transferring them on a cooling rack. You might break the freshly baked donuts if removed immediately as it still continues to cook in its inside.

- For baked donuts which you won't be able to consume, place them in a tightly sealed bag or jar to keep their freshness for days.
- Baked donuts sometimes seem to dry out quickly. You may want to soak it a while in a very thin glaze that is a mixture of about a cup of powdered sugar, 1 teaspoon of vanilla and 2 tablespoons of water/milk. Bathe the donuts with the glaze then let them set for few hours. This helps them seal up and retain more moisture.

LET'S GET STARTED

In *The Donut Cookbook,* you'll be able to take hold of an awesome variety of mouthwatering baked donuts. These donuts will be fun to make and will help to master the art of making the perfect homemade donuts.

Whatever you choose from this special collection of over 100 delicious baked donut recipes, it's totally up to you. Just follow the instructions in this book and the different methods of preparing and baking these donuts and it will become surprisingly simple. In some cases, feel free to make your own ingredient substitutions and tweak the recipes here and there based on your preferences or individual situations.

A lot of time has been spent in trying to bring these recipes to perfection, but sometimes it's impossible to catch it all. Therefore, if you find you don't like a particular ingredient, you may use a better or healthier substitute that is more to your liking whenever necessary. Just explore and enjoy!

Now, it's time to try your hand at making easy and yummy baked donuts using these specially developed donut recipes.

Happy baking!

4

BREAKFAST BITES DONUTS

Cinnamon Coated Donuts
This donut goes well with a cup of coffee at breakfast time. Enjoy the sweet coating which is well complimented with the pastry.

MAKES: 12 DONUTS
PREPARATION TIME: 2 hours, 15 minutes
BAKING TIME: 12 minutes

¾ cup strong white bread flour
1 rounded tablespoon caster sugar
1½ tablespoons butter, cut into small pieces
½ tablespoon easy-blend dried yeast
5 tablespoon milk
1 egg, beaten
4 tablespoons minced meat

For the Coating:
3 tablespoons icing sugar
6 tablespoons caster sugar

1 teaspoon cinnamon

Directions

1. Tip the flour, sugar and a good pinch of salt into a large bowl.
2. Add the butter and rub into the flour using fingertips.
3. Stir in the yeast.
4. Warm the milk to hand-hot temperature.
5. Make a well in the center of the flour and add the milk and egg.
6. Mix everything together to make a soft dough.
7. Tip onto a lightly floured surface and knead for 5 minutes until dough is elastic, smooth, and is no longer sticky.
8. Put the dough back in the bowl and cover it with a tea towel and leave to rise for about an hour or till it doubles in size.
9. Briefly knead the dough again, and then divide into 12 equal pieces.
10. Roll out each piece to a 9cm round and put 1 teaspoon mincemeat in the center.
11. Fold the edges of the dough to enclose the filling and pinch it well to enclose.
12. Shape batter in to a ball using your hands and put on a baking sheet lined with baking paper with sealed side down.
13. Allowing space for the dough to rise.
14. Cover it with a tea towel and leave for about 30 minutes.
15. Heat the oven to 190°F.
16. Bake donuts for 10-12 minutes until risen and golden.
17. Allow to cool for few minutes in the pan before transferring donuts on a cooling rack.
18. Roll each donut first in the sugar syrup, then into the caster sugar to coat it all over.

To assemble

1. Melt the icing sugar with 2 tablespoons cold water in a shallow bowl.
2. Mix the caster sugar and cinnamon in another bowl.

Apple Crisp Donuts

Why not try these apple crisp donuts this Fall. You will love the crispiness of these donuts with the aroma of cinnamon in every bite you make.

MAKES: 6 DONUTS
PREPARATION TIME: 10 minutes
BAKING TIME: 12 minutes

1 cup flour
½ cup agave
1 teaspoon baking powder
¼ teaspoon salt
½ cup soy yogurt
2 tablespoon vegetable or coconut oil
1 tablespoon apple cider vinegar
2 tablespoon almond milk

For the apple crisp:
½ cup small diced apples
1 teaspoon cinnamon
1 tablespoon vegan butter
1 tablespoon coconut sugar
1 tablespoon oats, mashed

Directions

1. Preheat oven to 375°F.
2. In a medium bowl, combine all dry ingredients.
3. In another medium bowl mix all wet ingredients well until smooth.
4. Combine wet and dry together and mix well.
5. Transfer batter to a large sealable bag and then cut one of its corners.
6. Pipe batter into each donut round, and smooth out with the back of a spoon if needed.
7. Bake in the oven for 10-12 minutes.
8. Remove from oven and allow cooling in pan for 5 minutes.
9. Turn donuts onto a cooling rack and allow to fully cool before glazing or dusting with powdered sugar.

To make the glaze

1. Combine all ingredients well then sprinkle into each donut mold before piping batter into the molds.

Vanilla Green Tea Donut

A good way to enjoy your favorite refreshing green tea is to have it in this delicious donut. Enjoy this Vanilla Green Tea Donut for breakfast or whenever you wish.

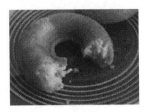

MAKES: 12 DONUTS
PREPARATION TIME: 5 minutes
BAKING TIME: 10 minutes

1 cup all-purpose flour
1/3 cup sugar
¾ teaspoon baking powder
¾ teaspoon baking soda
¼ teaspoon salt
½ teaspoon green tea powder
1 egg
½ cup plain yogurt
2 tablespoons milk
1 teaspoon vanilla extract
1 tablespoon canola oil

Directions

1. Preheat oven at 400°F.
2. In a big bowl, combine dry ingredients. Whisk and mix well.
3. Make a well in the center and add in all wet ingredients. Mix all thoroughly.

4. Spray the donut pan with nonstick cooking spray.
5. Divide batter among pan wells, placing only half full.
6. Bake for 10 minutes or until a toothpick inserted comes out clean.
7. Cool for 5 minutes before removing from pans then to a wire rack.

Buttermilk Pineapple Donuts

This scrumptious goody has the sweet-sour pineapple fruit taste and will make a treat that you surely won't regret.

MAKES: 6 DONUTS
PREPARATION TIME: 15 minutes
BAKING TIME: 12 minutes

¾ cups cake flour
1/3 cup sugar
1/3 teaspoon baking soda
1/3 teaspoon salt
¼ cup vegetable oil
¼ cup buttermilk
1/3 teaspoon rum extract
1 egg
1/3 teaspoon white vinegar
3 tablespoons crushed pineapple

For the Glaze
2 tablespoons crushed pineapple
½ cups confectioners' sugar
1½ tablespoons pineapple juice
½ cups shredded coconut

Directions

1. Preheat oven to 375° F.
2. Lightly coat donut pan with oil.
3. Mix together all dry ingredients and whisk to thoroughly combine ingredients.
4. In a separate bowl combine all dry ingredients, except for the vinegar. Whisk until well combined.
5. Combine the wet mixture to the dry and mix only until moistened.
6. Add vinegar, and mix well.
7. Gently fold in well-drained pineapples until combined.
8. Fill donut wells only until three-quarters full.
9. Bake for 10-12 minutes or until donuts turn golden brown.
10. Let cool in pan for 5 minutes.
11. Transfer donuts out onto a wire rack to cool completely.
12. Spoon glaze onto cooled donuts.
13. Sprinkle coconut immediately.
14. Return glazed donuts to wire rack to set.

To make the Glaze
1. Mix pineapple, sugar and pineapple juice in a mixing bowl until it becomes smooth and creamy.

Kefir Berry Donuts

These healthy and nutrient-filled kefir donuts are a must-try for everyone. These donuts are delicately hand-dipped in luscious homemade berry icing.

MAKES: 12 DONUTS
PREPARATION TIME: 10 minutes
BAKING TIME: 9 minutes

2 cups all-purpose flour
½ cup sugar
1½ teaspoons baking powder
½ teaspoon freshly ground nutmeg
½ teaspoon salt
¾ cup kefir
2 large eggs
¼ cup honey
2 tablespoons melted butter
½ teaspoon vanilla extract

Berry Icing:
½ cup frozen mixed berries
2 tablespoons of sugar
1½ cups powdered sugar
½ teaspoon vanilla

Directions

2. Preheat oven to 425°F.
3. Lightly grease a donut pan.
4. Combine flours and next 4 ingredients in a large bowl, stirring well using a whisk.
5. Combine kefir, eggs, butter, honey, and vanilla, stirring well.
6. Add wet mixture to flour mixture then whisk just until well combined.
7. Spoon batter into donut pans, filling two thirds full each.
8. Bake in the middle of oven for 9 minutes or until donuts spring back when touched and are golden on bottom.
9. Let cool in pan slightly then turn out onto a wire rack.

For the Icing

1. Cook berries with sugar and a couple tablespoons of water over medium heat until the berries are cooked down to a sauce for about 15 minutes. Strain it into a bowl to get rid of any seeds then add the powdered sugar and vanilla extract. Mix them well.
2. Dip each cooled donut into the icing then return to the rack to set.

Coconut Oat Topped Donuts

These healthy coconut donuts are baked into goodness. These are also topped with the sweet combination of syrup, coconut, and hearty oats.

MAKES: 10 DONUTS
PREPARATION TIME: 5 minutes
BAKING TIME: 8 minutes

1½ cups plain flour
½ cup brown sugar
½ cup desiccated coconut
1½ teaspoons baking powder
½ cup rolled oats
¾ cup low-fat milk
1 egg
8 tablespoons melted butter
1 tablespoon golden syrup

Glaze:
icing sugar
boiling water, enough amount to make a thin syrup

Topping:
pan toasted desiccated coconut
rolled oats
golden syrup

Directions

1. Preheat oven to 350°F.
2. Combine all dry ingredients together in a mixing bowl and make a well.
3. Whisk wet ingredients together and then pour and combine with dry ingredients to make the batter.
4. Spray donut pan with cooking oil spray.
5. Carefully spoon batter into pan.
6. Bake donuts for around 8 minutes.
7. Cool in pan for few minutes before removing donuts on wire rack.
8. Prepare topping in a frying pan. Set it aside.

To make the glaze

1. Just dissolve icing with boiling water.
2. Drizzle over cooled donuts, quickly sprinkle topping.
3. Refrigerate to set.

Banana Carrot Donut

Enjoy these donuts which are not as sweet and as heavy as the usual carrot cake. This goes well with a glass of chocolate drink.

MAKES: 6 DONUTS
PREPARATION TIME: 5 minutes
BAKING TIME: 10 minutes

1/3 cup whole wheat flour
1/3 cup all-purpose flour
¾ tablespoons wheat germ
pinch of salt
3 tablespoons sugar
1/3 teaspoon baking powder
1/8 teaspoon baking soda
1/3 teaspoon pumpkin pie spice
1 large egg
3 tablespoons cup canola oil
3 tablespoons baby food carrot puree
½ of a medium banana, mashed
3 tablespoons plain yogurt
1/3 cup grated carrots

Directions

1. Heat oven to 350°F.
2. Spray a standard donut pan with non-stick cooking spray.

3. Combine the first 8 ingredients in a large bowl.
4. Whisk eggs, oil, banana, baby-food carrots, and yogurt in a separate bowl.
5. Gently stir the liquid ingredients into the dry mixture.
6. Stir in the grated carrots.
7. Place batter in a piping bag.
8. Evenly fill each well in the donut pan to 3/4 full.

Butternut Donuts with Vanilla Icing

Enjoy your day with a classic donut breakfast. With butternut in the dough, and a simple vanilla icing, this decadent donut is a great way to start your day.

MAKES: 6 DONUTS
PREPARATION TIME: 5 minutes
BAKING TIME: 8 minutes

---

6 tablespoons all-purpose flour
½ cup sugar
½ teaspoon baking soda
½ teaspoon ground nutmeg
½ cup mashed or canned butternut squash
2 eggs
½ teaspoon vanilla extract

Vanilla Icing:
1 cup powdered sugar
½ teaspoon light corn syrup
½ teaspoon vanilla extract
pinch of kosher salt
1 tablespoon hot water

Directions

1. Preheat oven to 375° F.
2. Coat a 6-cavity Donut Pan with cooking spray.
3. In a medium bowl, combine sugar, flour, nutmeg and

baking soda. Whisk to aerate and blend.

4. In a separate bowl, beat eggs and stir in vanilla and squash. Slowly fold wet ingredients into dry ingredients mixture until just combined.
5. Pipe batter into prepared donut pan.
6. Bake for 7-8 minutes or until an inserted toothpick comes out clean.
7. Let cool directly in the pan.
8. Release from pan with a spoon.

For the icing

1. Mix all ingredients and drizzle in stripes to the top of each donut. You can use a piping bag with a fine tip or a spoon to do this.

Morning Wheat-Free Donuts

Grab a bite and enjoy a wheat-free donut. This delightful donut is best with a cup of coffee and fresh fruit for your breakfast meal.

MAKES: 6 DONUTS
PREPARATION TIME: 10 minutes
BAKING TIME: 15 minutes

¼ cup buckwheat flour
¼ cup potato starch
¼ cup sweet white rice flour
¼ cup sweet white sorghum
½ cup sugar or ¼ cup agave
½ teaspoon xanthan
1 teaspoon baking powder
¼ teaspoon salt
¼ teaspoon gluten-free baking soda
1/8 cup canola oil
½ cup rice milk
1 teaspoon vanilla extract
3 tablespoons unsweetened applesauce

Directions

1. Preheat oven at 350° F
2. Whisk together all of the dry ingredients in a bowl.
3. Whisk together all the wet ingredients in another bowl

then gradually stir into the bowl of dry mixture.

4. Stir until everything in the donut batter is completely combined.
5. Pour the donut batter into a batter dispenser or a durable plastic bag then cut a small opening in one end.
6. Pipe the donut batter into oiled donut tins.
7. Bake for 15 minutes. Serve.

Old-Fashioned Spiced Donuts

Nothing beats freshly baked donuts for a midday nibble or even for breakfast. You're free to add your desired frosting or toppings on this sumptuous old-fashioned donut.

MAKES: 6 DONUTS
PREPARATION TIME: 5 minutes
BAKING TIME: 9 minutes

Non-stick vegetable pan spray
1 cup cake flour, sifted
6 tablespoons granulated sugar
1 teaspoon baking powder
pinch ground nutmeg
pinch salt
6 tablespoons buttermilk
1 egg, lightly beaten
1 tablespoon butter, melted

Directions

1. Preheat oven to 425°F.
2. Spray donut pan with vegetable cooking spray.
3. In large bowl, mix together flour, sugar, nutmeg and salt, and baking powder.
4. Form a well in the center of the mixture and add eggs, buttermilk, and the butter.
5. Beat until just combined.

6. Fill each pan cavity approximately 2/3 full.
7. Bake 7-9 minutes or until the tops of the donuts pushes back when touched.
8. Let cool in pan for 5 minutes before removing.

Sugary Cinnamon Blueberry Donuts

Try these easy and delicious baked blueberry donuts coated with melted butter, sugar and cinnamon. These donuts are also great for breakfasts and easily loved.

MAKES: 6 DONUTS
PREPARATION TIME: 10 minutes
BAKING TIME: 20 minutes

---

1 cup whole wheat pastry flour
¼ cup sugar
1 egg
1 cup of fresh blueberries
½ teaspoon baking powder
¼ teaspoon baking soda
½ cup low-fat milk
1 tablespoons olive oil
½ teaspoon vanilla
pinch cinnamon
pinch nutmeg

For the sugar coating
1½ tablespoons of melted butter
¼ cup sugar
½ tablespoon of cinnamon

Directions

1. Preheat oven to 325°F.
2. Spray donut pan with cooking oil.
3. In a bowl, whisk milk, eggs, sugar, vanilla, oil, nutmeg and cinnamon.
4. Add in flour, baking powder and baking soda then whisk until combined.
5. Slowly fold in blueberries.
6. Spoon in batter to fill each donut hole up to 2/3 full.
7. Bake for 15-20 minutes. Cool for about 5 minutes and remove from pan to a wire rack. Let them cool there completely.

For the topping

1. In a bowl, combine sugar and cinnamon. Place melted butter in a wide-mouthed bowl.
2. Dip each donut on the butter then followed by the cinnamon sugar.

Walnut Streusel Cake Donuts

These are heavenly scented cake donuts topped with divine walnut streusel. This is a perfect treat for your morning meal with a cold glass of milk.

MAKES: 6 DONUTS
PREPARATION TIME: 10 minutes
BAKING TIME: 8 minutes

---

2 cups all-purpose flour
1 teaspoon baking powder
¼ teaspoon nutmeg
½ teaspoon cinnamon
½ teaspoon salt
2 large eggs
¾ cup granulated sugar
1 teaspoon vanilla
½ cup milk
2 tablespoons butter, melted

Walnut Streusel Topping
½ cup all-purpose flour
4 tablespoons of a firmly-packed brown sugar
½ teaspoon ground cinnamon
pinch of kosher salt
2 tablespoons cold unsalted butter
2 tablespoons chopped walnuts

Directions

1. Preheat the oven to 325°F.
2. Grease a baked donut pan.
3. Combine the spices, flour, salt, baking powder in a large mixing bowl.
4. Whisk together the eggs with the sugar, vanilla, melted butter and milk in a large mixing bowl.
5. Add the liquid mixture to the dry mixture a third at a time, stirring continuously after each addition.
6. Stir until the batter is smooth.
7. **Prepare the streusel topping:** Pulse the flour, brown sugar, cinnamon, salt and butter in a food processor until the butter is about a pea-sized. Stir in the walnuts.
8. Fill the donut wells to 2/3 full of batter. Sprinkle the topping over the batter in the donut pan.
9. Bake for 8 minutes.
10. Cool for several minutes in the pan and then remove the donuts using a silicone spatula to transfer and completely cool on a rack.

Morning French Style Donuts

Preparation Time: 5 Minutes
Baking Time: 20 Minutes
Makes: 6 Donuts

---

5 tablespoons Unsalted Butter (cooled to room temperature)
½ cup Light Brown Sugar
1 Large Egg, beaten
1½ cups All-Purpose White Flour
2¼ teaspoons Baking Powder
¼ teaspoons Salt
½ teaspoon Grated Nutmeg
½ cup Milk
Nonstick Cooking Spray

Topping Ingredients
3 tablespoons melted Unsalted Butter
¼-1/2 cup White Sugar
1 tablespoon Cinnamon Powder

Directions

1. Preheat oven to 350 degrees Fahrenheit. Prepare a nonstick 6-cavity donut pan with cooking spray then place it aside.
2. Mix together the unsalted butter and light brown sugar until a fluffy and creamy mixture is achieved. Add in the egg and combine thoroughly.
3. Sift the following dry ingredients together: baking powder, all-purpose flour, grated nutmeg and salt. Alternately fold in the dry ingredients with the milk.
4. Use a piping bag to evenly pipe the donut batter in each cavity in the pan about half full.

5. Allow to the batter to bake for approximately 20 minutes.

6. In the meantime, place the melted butter in a medium bowl, then combine the white sugar and the cinnamon powder in another medium bowl. Place both bowls aside.

7. After the baking time for the doughnuts are completed, remove the pan straightaway and swirl the top of each donut, first into the melted butter, then next into the white sugar and cinnamon powder mixture. Serve as you like.

Vegan Espresso Donuts

Enjoy the inviting aroma of strong coffee on your pastry. Prepare these espresso donuts and have a coffee blast.

MAKES: 12 DONUTS
PREPARATION TIME: 2 hours 30 minutes
BAKING TIME: 10 minutes

4½ cups flour
2 cups soy milk, light vanilla flavor
1/3 cup maple syrup
1/3 cup oil
½ cup sugar
1 package active dry yeast
1 teaspoon salt

Espresso glaze
4 cups powdered sugar
3 tablespoons quality espresso

Streusel topping:
½ cup brown sugar
4 tablespoons butter, non-dairy
3 tablespoons flour

Directions

1. Mix oil, soy milk, maple syrup, and sugar in a small sauce pan and bring to a boil.
2. Remove from heat and set aside for 30 minutes to cool until lukewarm (110° F). Stir in yeast and let set for 10 minutes.
3. In a large bowl, mix flour and salt, then add to liquid mixture and mixing well, then cover with a towel and let rise in a warm place for 1 hour.
4. Once dough doubled in size, add the remaining ½ cup of flour or until it is no longer extremely sticky. Mix well and then let it sit for another 10 minutes.
5. Mold 2-inch balls on a floured surface and place them on a lightly greased cookie sheet, leaving room for expansion for each.
6. Preheat oven to 350°F and cover with light towel while warming.
7. Bake for 10 -11 minutes. Make sure not to over bake, you don't want the bottoms to be too brown.
8. Prepare glaze and streusel. Once donuts are done, let them cool a bit and then dunk in glaze and cover with streusel. Consider adding streusel in the bottoms for better flavor.
9. Serve immediately. You may store it in an air-tight container for up to 2 days.

Notes

For the streusel add brown sugar and flour gradually until you achieve your desired texture. It's best if it is of a crumbly texture but not too dry or buttery.

Raisin Yogurt Cake Donuts

Having raisins in your donut is surely sweet and yummy treat. Enjoy this delicious donut for lunch or breakfast.

MAKES: 6 DONUTS
PREPARATION TIME: 5 minutes
BAKING TIME: 10 minutes

---

1 cup all-purpose flour
1/3 cup white granulated sugar
¾ teaspoon baking powder
¾ teaspoon baking soda
¼ teaspoon salt
1 large egg
1 tub (6 ounces) plain yogurt
1 tablespoon canola oil
1 teaspoon pure vanilla extract
1/3 cup dried raisins

Directions

1. Preheat oven at 400°F.
2. In a big glass bowl, combine dry ingredients, except the raisins. Whisk thoroughly using a whisk.
3. In the center, add in all wet ingredients. Whisk until thoroughly combined.
4. Add raisins and mix well.

5. Spoon batter and fill the greased donut pan.
6. Bake 10 minutes.
7. Remove donuts using a thin silicone spatula and cool on wire rack.

Apple-Vegan Rounds

The sweet smell and unique taste of apples and cinnamon is incredibly perfect. You'll surely savor it with each bite of this apple vegan donut.

MAKES: 6 DONUTS
PREPARATION TIME: 10 minutes
BAKING TIME: 12 minutes

---

1 cup all-purpose flour
1½ teaspoons baking powder
½ cup sugar
¼ teaspoon nutmeg
1 tiny pinch of cinnamon
¼ teaspoons salt
½ cup soymilk
½ teaspoon apple cider vinegar
4 tablespoons non-dairy butter
½ teaspoon pure vanilla extract
¼ cup applesauce, as replacement for 1 egg
Any topping or glaze of your choice

Directions

1. Combine all dry ingredients in a large bowl using a whisk to mix thoroughly. Combine and heat all wet ingredients in a small sauce pan over medium low heat

and mix until butter is melted. This mixture shouldn't get too hot; you should be able to stick your finger in the mixture.

2. Add wet to dry mixture and mix until perfectly combined and forms a very soft dough.
3. Using a tablespoon, scoop out dough into an ungreased nonstick donut pan. Smooth out the top of the dough using fingers to make more even and prettier donuts.
4. Preheat oven to 350° F.
5. Bake for 12 minutes. They should not be browned on top, but a tester will come out clean. Turn over the hot donut pan to release the donuts in a cooling rack. Allow it to cool a bit then decorate.

Banana Chocolate Chip Donut Cakes

Having a hard time choosing between bananas and chocolate? Well, if you do, then this is your chance to munch both in one donut cake pastry.

MAKES: 12 DONUTS
PREPARATION TIME: 15 minutes
BAKING TIME: 15 minutes

---

1 cup mashed ripe banana
½ cup raw cane sugar
½ cup fat-free Greek yogurt
¼ cup unsalted butter
2 Eggs
1 teaspoon pure vanilla extract
2 cups spelt white flours
1 teaspoon baking powder
½ teaspoon baking soda
¼ teaspoon salt
½ cup dark chocolate chips
½ cup milk chocolate chips

For the Glaze:
¼ cup milk
1 teaspoon rose extract
3 cups confectionary sugar, sifted
a few drops of white wine
a choice of decorations

Directions

1. Preheat the oven to 325°F.
2. Using an electric mixer with the whisk attachment, add the mashed banana, Greek yogurt, and sugar. Mix until incorporated.
3. Add melted butter, eggs and vanilla extract then mix it well.
4. Now add flour, baking powder, salt, and baking soda to the batter and mix until just incorporated.
5. Do not over mix it.
6. Using a spatula, fold in the chocolate chips.
7. Scoop the batter into a pastry bag and seal it. Snip the bottom corner of the bag.
8. Grease the donut baking pan.
9. Pipe ¾ full of the batter into each donut mold.
10. Bake for about 12 to 15 minutes.
11. Remove from the pan and allow it to cool there for a while before placing on a cooling rack.

For the glaze

1. The glaze dries fast so you need to work fast. Make sure to have everything set up beforehand. Split the decorations into small wide bowls each for 1 kind. In a double boiler, heat milk and rose extract over medium heat. Slowly stir in the sugar until a smooth glaze is formed. Add the food coloring and stir until mixed in well. Adjust the heat down to low.
2. One at a time, dip the donuts in the glaze; hold the dipped donuts over the pan to drip off the excess glaze.
3. Immediately dip the glazed donut into the decorations.
4. Place back on the rack to set.

Topless Dough Rings

The good thing on baking plain donuts is the fun you get in choosing toppings. Enjoy the exciting experience with these rings.

MAKES: 6 DONUTS
PREPARATION TIME: 10 minutes
BAKING TIME: 17 minutes

½ cup coconut flour
½ cup arrowroot flour or coconut flour
1 teaspoon baking soda
1 teaspoon baking powder
6 tablespoons coconut sugar
2 teaspoons vanilla extract
¾ cup unsweetened apple sauce
2 tablespoons almond milk , unsweetened

Directions

1. Preheat oven to 325°F.
2. Mix all dry ingredients in a bowl. Then add in the wet and mix everything well.
3. Spoon batter into your donut pan. Grease it if you're not using a non-stick pan.
4. Bake in the oven for around 15-17 minutes.

Cinnamon and Pumpkin Donuts

Pumpkin gives good color and texture to these donuts. Plus it also fortifies them with vitamin A and antioxidants.

MAKES: 6 DONUTS
PREPARATION TIME: 15 minutes
BAKING TIME: 12 minutes

---

1 cup flour
1 teaspoon baking powder
pinch of freshly grated nutmeg
pinch of ground cloves
pinch of baking soda
½ ripe banana, well-mashed
½ cup pumpkin puree
pinch of teaspoon salt
2 teaspoons cinnamon
2 tablespoons oil, plus some for greasing donut pan
3 tablespoons maple syrup
1½ tablespoons almond milk

Glaze:
½ teaspoon cinnamon
2 tablespoons almond milk
1¼ cups powdered sugar
1 tablespoon maple syrup
Any sprinkles or any non-dairy for decorations

Directions

2. Preheat the oven to 350° F.
3. Mix the dry donut ingredients using a large bowl.
4. Mix the wet ingredients in a separate bowl. Then combine the two mixtures and stir just until all are thoroughly combined.
5. Grease the donut pan wells, and then fill them with batter almost up to the top.
6. Bake until fluffy and golden for about 12 minutes or until it bounces back when poked. Then move the tray on a cooling rack.
7. Cool in the pan for about ten minutes, and then carefully use a butter knife to circle around the edges and gently remove each donut out of the pan and onto the rack. Let the donuts cool completely.

For the glaze

1. Mix ingredients in a bowl. It should have a good spreading consistency, but thin enough to still drip. Add powdered sugar or milk one tablespoon at a time to adjust the consistency.
2. Lay the donuts out on wax paper and use a spoon to spread the glaze on each donut.
3. Apply sprinkles or desired toppings while the glaze is still wet, and then leave them on the wax paper for glaze to set.

Creamy Nectarine Minis

Enjoy these soft and creamy baked mini gluten-free donuts. The nectarines give a perfect tanginess of these fun-sized donuts.

MAKES: 24 MINI DONUTS
PREPARATION TIME: 10 minutes
BAKING TIME: 15 minutes

1 cup gluten-free flour of your choice
1 teaspoon xanthan gum
½ cup caster sugar
1 teaspoon gluten-free baking powder
¼ teaspoon salt
1 teaspoon vanilla extract
1 fresh nectarine, pureed
2 large eggs
3 tablespoons vegetable oil
2 tablespoons buttermilk

Directions

1. Preheat oven to 370° F.
2. Lightly spray donut pan with non-stick cooking spray.
3. In a mixing bowl, whisk together all wet ingredients, except for puree, until you get a foamy mixture.
4. Add in the sifted dry ingredients to the wet mixture and

5. mix until combined.
6. Stir pureed nectarine in to mixture.
7. Pipe batter into greased donut pan until each cavity is ¾ full.
8. Bake for 10-15 minutes or until donut springs back when lightly pressed.
9. Remove from oven and let it cool for 5 minutes then transfer onto a cooling rack.

CHOCOLATE HAVEN DONUTS

Baked Chocolate Frosted Cake Donuts

It's impossible to say "No" to this tempting chocolate frosted pastry. Its oozing chocolate is calling out for a yummy bite!

MAKES: 12 DONUTS
PREPARATION TIME: 10 minutes
BAKING TIME: 20 minutes

---

1 cup plain flour
1/3 cup caster sugar
1 teaspoon baking powder
¼ cup milk
3 tablespoons butter, melted
1 egg, lightly whisked
6 tablespoons dark chocolate, finely chopped
½ cup thickened cream

Directions

1. Preheat oven to 350°F.
2. Combine flour, sugar and baking powder in a mixing bowl. Make a well at the center and stir in milk, butter and egg until it becomes smooth.
3. Spoon batter into a sealable plastic bag. Cut 1 corner of the bag to make a hole.
4. Pipe evenly to 12-count or two 6-count donut pan.
5. Bake for 18-20 minutes or until a skewer inserted into donuts comes out clean.
6. Cool for 5 minutes before removing from pans then to a wire rack.

For frosting

1. Whisk chocolate and cream in a saucepan over medium heat for 5 minutes or until smooth. Then set aside for 20 minutes to thicken.
2. Dip the lighter side of donuts into the chocolate mixture.
3. Place glazed donuts on a tray to set.

Choco-Hazelnut Glazed Banana Donuts

There's a perfect combination in this donut. The creamy chocolate hazelnut butter frosting and the fresh banana in the dough makes it a great dessert unlike any other.

MAKES: 12 DONUTS
PREPARATION TIME: 10 minutes
BAKING TIME: 18 minutes

½ cup sugar
1 cup unbleached all-purpose flour
2 teaspoons gluten-free baking powder
¼ teaspoon salt
½ cup buttermilk
½ cup very ripe banana, mashed
¼ cup sour cream
2 tablespoons butter, melted
1 teaspoon vanilla extract
1 large egg

For the glaze:
¼ cup chocolate hazelnut butter
1/8 cup milk

Directions

1. Preheat the oven to 350°F.
2. In a medium bowl, combine the flour, baking powder,

salt, and sugar.

3. In a 2-cup measuring bowl, whisk together buttermilk, vanilla extract, egg, and butter.
4. Whisk together wet ingredients.
5. Wet goes into dry, stir well to combine all.
6. Fold in the mashed banana, making sure it's evenly distributed in the batter.
7. Stir in the sour cream.
8. Lightly oil your donut molds and fill each well with batter.
9. Bake for 15 to 18 minutes, or until a toothpick inserted into a donut comes out clean.
10. Remove the pan from the oven and let it cool completely.

For the glaze

1. Whisk together the chocolate hazelnut butter and milk using a fork, until the consistency is smooth and creamy.
2. Fit a baking rack over a cookie sheet, and then flip your donut pan over it to release all the donuts.
3. Dip each donut into the glaze and let it drip dry back on the baking rack.

Minty Chocolate Donut

We know that chocolate and mint has been matched for quite a while now. So having a minty chocolate donut with your is absolutely not a bad idea after all.

MAKES: 12 DONUTS
PREPARATION TIME: 10 minutes
BAKING TIME: 9 minutes

---

1 cup cake flour
1 teaspoon baking powder
¼ cup unsweetened cocoa powder
½ cup sugar
2 tablespoons butter
½ cup buttermilk
1 egg
½ cup fresh mint leaves, minced

Chocolate glaze:
3 tablespoons cream
¼ cup of finely chopped semi-sweet chocolate
1 tablespoon corn syrup
1 cup powdered sugar

Directions

1.   Preheat the oven to 325°F.

2. Prepare a donut pan with baking spray.
3. Combine all of the dry ingredients in a medium sized bowl.
4. Melt the butter in a small sauce pan over medium heat.
5. While the butter is melting, whisk together the buttermilk and eggs in a small bowl.
6. Add the buttermilk mixture to the dry ingredients and mix them well.
7. Stir in the melted butter.
8. Add the mint to the batter and mix well.
9. Spoon the batter into the donut pan.
10. Bake for 10 minutes.
11. Let cool for a minute before turning out onto a cooling rack.
12. Bake the remaining batter and let them cool as well.

For the chocolate glaze

1. Simmer cream. Combine all of the other ingredients in a medium bowl and pour the hot cream over the mixture. Whisk it until shiny and smooth.
2. Dunk each donut half way in the glaze and twist to drip off excess glaze.
3. Place back on the cooling rack for glaze to set up.

Chocolate Donut Holes with Creamy Lemon Glaze

Bake these for your kids this weekend and you'll surely get hugs and kisses from them. No doubt they will love the lemony taste that mixes with the chocolate.

MAKES: 12 DONUT Holes
PREPARATION TIME: 10 minutes
BAKING TIME: 10 minutes

---

1 cup white whole wheat
½ granulated sugar
4 tablespoons cocoa powder, unsweetened
½ teaspoon baking powder
½ teaspoon baking soda
pinch of salt
1 large egg, beaten
6 tablespoons milk
2 tablespoons Greek yogurt
1 teaspoon vanilla extract
1½ tablespoons unsalted butter

Glaze:
¾ cup confectioners' sugar
2 tablespoons heavy cream
½ teaspoon vanilla extract
½ teaspoon lemon juice

Directions

1. Preheat oven to 350 F degrees.
2. Spray 12-count mini muffin pan with nonstick spray.
3. Sift flour, sugar, and cocoa powder together in a mixing large bowl.
4. Mix in the baking soda, baking powder, salt. Leave it aside.
5. In a medium bowl, whisk the beaten eggs, milk, and vanilla yogurt together until completely smoothens.
6. Whisk in the butter until combined.
7. Gradually fold the wet ingredients into the dry ingredients. Mix the two together only until no flour lumps remain.
8. Spoon batter into the mini muffin tins, only about ¾ full.
9. Bake for 10 minutes, or until a toothpick inserted in the center comes out clean. Do not over-bake them; they burn easily.
10. Allow the donuts to cool for 5 minutes in the pan and then transfer to a wire rack to cool for 5 more minutes before glazing them.

To make the glaze

1. Sift the confectioner's sugar into a medium bowl. Stir in the milk, lemon juice, and vanilla until smooth and well combined. Add more confectioners' sugar to make it thicker; add more cream to make it thinner.
2. Dunk each slightly warm donut hole into the glaze.
3. Place on a wire rack on top of a large baking sheet to let the glaze drip down on it. Repeat dunking two to three more times if you desire a thick glaze coating.

Trio Choco Baked Donuts

Chocolate dough, chocolate frost, and chocolate sprinkles all in one good looking donut. That's what Trio Choco is all about.

MAKES: 6 DONUTS
PREPARATION TIME: 10 minutes
BAKING TIME: 15 minutes

3 tablespoons cocoa powder, good quality
½ cup all-purpose flour
7 tablespoons light brown sugar
1/3 teaspoon baking powder
pinch of espresso powder
1/3 teaspoon baking soda
small pinch of salt
6 tablespoons chocolate chips
1 egg
4 tablespoons milk
¾ teaspoon vanilla extract
¾ teaspoon vinegar, cider
3 tablespoons melted butter

Chocolate Glaze:
1/3 cup chocolate chips
2 tablespoons half & half cream
Chocolate sprinkles

Directions

1. Preheat the oven to 350°F.
2. Lightly grease the wells of a standard donut pan.
3. In a large bowl, whisk together all dry ingredients then set aside.
4. In a large measuring cup or medium-sized mixing bowl, whisk wet ingredients.
5. Add the wet ingredients to the dry ingredients, stirring thoroughly to blend.
6. Spoon the batter into the prepared pan filling them to ¾ full.
7. Bake the donuts for 13 to 15 minutes or until a toothpick inserted into the center of one comes out clean.
8. Remove the donuts from the oven, and after a minute or so, loosen their edges.
9. Turn the pan upside down above a rack, and gently let the donuts fall.
10. Allow them to cool completely.

To make the glaze

1. Combine the chocolate chips and half & half in a microwave-safe bowl. Heat it in 20 second increments. Stir the mixture in between until you achieve a smooth consistency. Remove from the microwave, and stir until the chips have melted and the glaze turns smooth.
2. Spread glaze on the donuts using a spoon.
3. Sprinkle with chocolate sprinkles.

Mini Chocolate-Pumpkin Mallow Donuts

The marsh mallows look pretty good on these tiny but incredibly delicious donuts. These are great snacks for your kids' play dates.

MAKES: 15 MINI DONUTS
PREPARATION TIME: 10 minutes
BAKING TIME: 9 minutes

2 tablespoons plus 1 tablespoon brown sugar
¼ teaspoon baking powder
½ cup white whole wheat flour
¼ teaspoon baking soda
1/8 teaspoon salt
5 tablespoons cocoa powder
½ teaspoon pumpkin pie spice
¼ cup almond milk
¼ cup canned pumpkin
1 egg
½ teaspoon vanilla extract
½ teaspoon apple cider vinegar

Chocolate and mallows topping:
3 tablespoons dark chocolate chips
1½ tablespoons pumpkin spice creamer
Small marshmallows

Directions

1. Preheat the oven to 350°F.
2. Spray the wells of a 24-count mini donut pan with cooking spray.
3. Whisk together the all dry ingredients in a large mixing bowl. Set it aside afterwards.
4. In a medium bowl, whisk together the wet ingredients.
5. Add the wet ingredients to the dry mixture and stir until ingredients are well combined.
6. Scoop the batter into a large pastry bag. Trim a hole at a corner of the bag to pipe the batter out into the donut well. Filling 15 wells at ¾ full in each.
7. Bake for 7-9 minutes, until a tester comes out clean.
8. Remove donuts from oven and after about cool slightly before turning them out onto the cooling rack.

For the topping

1. Combine the chocolate chips and creamer in a small saucepan and heat in the microwave oven with 30 second intervals for 1 minute until melted. Stir it every 30 seconds.
2. Dip each donut into glaze then decorate with mallows.

Coffee Chocolate Cake Donuts

For those times you want to have a nice but not too overly chocolaty snack, these coffee chocolates are just what you need. Go grab the whisk and start baking!

MAKES: 6 DONUTS
PREPARATION TIME: 5 minutes
BAKING TIME: 13 minutes

---

1 cup all-purpose flour or extra ¼ cup if batter is too loose
¼ cup unsweetened cocoa powder
½ teaspoon baking soda
¼ teaspoon salt
½ cup milk
½ cup packed brown sugar
1 egg
4 teaspoons butter, melted
2 tablespoons coffee
1 teaspoon vanilla extract

For the glaze:
1 cup confectioners' sugar
2 tablespoons hot water
½ teaspoon almond extract

Directions

1. Heat oven to 325°F.
2. Coat donut pan with a non-stick cooking spray.
3. In large bowl, whisk all dry ingredients.
4. In small bowl, whisk all wet ingredients until smooth.
5. Combine both mixtures until blended and smooth.
6. Fill each donut cup approximately ¾ full.
7. Bake for 13 minutes or until donuts spring back when touched.
8. Allow to cool slightly before removing from pan.

To make glaze

1. Blend confectioners' sugar, hot water and extract in a small mixing bowl.
2. Dip each donut in the glaze and then top them with sprinkles.

Coco Choco Delight Donuts

Coco choco looks like the regular coconut topped donut, but it isn't. Unlike the ordinary, this donut uses nonfat milk and semi-sweet chocolate chips that turns into a low fat donut.

MAKES: 6 DONUTS
PREPARATION TIME: 5 minutes
BAKING TIME: 15 minutes

---

1 egg
½ cup non-fat milk
1 tablespoon olive oil
1 cup whole wheat flour
2 tablespoons cocoa powder
4 tablespoons sugar
½ teaspoon baking powder
¼ teaspoon baking soda
¼ cup semi-sweet chocolate chips

Glaze:
½ cup cacao chocolate chips
Grated coconut flakes, toasted

Directions

1. Preheat oven to 325°F.
2. In a large bowl mix the wet ingredients until well

combined.
3. Add remaining dry ingredients.
4. Mix it well; batter should be a little thick.
5. Spray donut pans with cooking spray.
6. Evenly spread batter into pans.
7. Bake for 15 minutes.
8. Let cool in pans for 3 minutes then transfer donuts to a wire rack to let them cool.

For the glaze:

1. In a double broiler, melt chocolate chips over medium heat until melted.
2. Dip donuts in warm melted chocolate
3. Sprinkle coconut on top.

Walnut Chocolate Donut

Chopped walnuts give a different texture and nutty aroma on these baked donuts. Plus, by covering the donut with lots of icing sugar it intensifies the goodness.

MAKES: 6 DONUTS
PREPARATION TIME: 5 minutes
BAKING TIME: 7 minutes

1 cup whole wheat flour
1 tablespoons baking powder
¼ teaspoon salt
¼ cup coconut sugar
¼ cup cocoa powder
1 teaspoon vanilla powder
¼ cup walnuts, coarsely chopped
¼ cup plus 2 tablespoons more almond milk
2 tablespoons orange juice
1 egg
3 tablespoons unsweetened applesauce
1 tablespoon canola oil
icing sugar

Directions

1.   Preheat oven to 450°F.

2. Grease donut pan.
3. In a large bowl, sift together dry ingredients except walnuts.
4. Stir in walnuts.
5. Add remaining dry ingredients and mix well.
6. Pipe equally into wells of donut pan.
7. Bake for 7 minutes.
8. Let the donuts rest for 2-3 minutes in the pan and then carefully remove them and transfer to a cooling rack after. You may use a spatula to help them out.
9. In a sealable bag, add some icing sugar.
10. Add one at a time donut in the bag.
11. Seal bag and then shake until donut is well coated. Do this just before eating the donuts to avoid the sugar to be absorbed by the dough.

Choc-o-Loco Overload Donuts

How sweet can you get with this chocolate overload donut! It's got chocolate dough, chocolate chips, and chocolate glaze.

MAKES: 12 DONUTS
PREPARATION TIME: 22 minutes
BAKING TIME: 22 minutes

½ cup oat flour
½ cup sweet rice flour
½ cup pure cane sugar
¼ cup unsweetened cocoa powder
2 tablespoons almond meal
2 tablespoons coconut flour
2 tablespoons ground flax meal
1 teaspoon baking powder
½ teaspoon baking soda
½ teaspoon salt
¾ cup unsweetened almond milk
¼ cup unsweetened applesauce
3 tablespoons grapeseed
½ cup 70% cocoa dark chocolate chips

For the Chocolate Frosting:
2-3 tablespoons almond milk, unsweetened
2/3 cup powdered sugar
3 tablespoons vegan butter
¼ cup cocoa powder
Vegan sprinkles

Directions

1. Preheat oven to 350°F.
2. Grease a donut pan.
3. Combine all dry ingredients in a large bowl and stir until combined.
4. In another bowl, whisk all of the wet ingredients until fully combined.
5. Pour the wet mixture into the dry ingredients and stir with a wooden spatula until just combined. Then let the batter sit for 5 minutes.
6. Spoon the batter into the donut wells, filling to just below the top of each mold from the top.
7. Lightly smooth out the top of the batter with a small silicone spatula but not pack the batter down.
8. Bake for 18-22 minutes. A toothpick inserted into the center should come out clean, unless it's the chocolate. Let cool in the pan for 5 minutes.
9. Slide a thin spatula around the edges of the donut to help loosen them out.
10. Then place on a cooling rack and allow to cool before topping.

For the frosting

1. Add all the frosting ingredients into a medium bowl and beat with electric mixer until smooth, adjusting the milk or sugar, if needed.
2. Spread the frosting onto cooled donuts and garnish with sprinkles.

Dark Chocolate Frosted Pumpkin Cake Rings

A duet of two chocolates on the frosting of this pumpkin donut makes it extra scrumptious. And the pumpkin puree fortifies it with nutrients as well.

MAKES: 6 DONUTS
PREPARATION TIME: 5 minutes
BAKING TIME: 8 minutes

½ cup sugar
6 tablespoons all-purpose flour
1 teaspoon pumpkin pie spice
½ teaspoon baking soda
½ cup canned pumpkin
1 large egg
½ teaspoon vanilla extract

Dark Chocolate Frosting:
2 tablespoons sugar
2 tablespoons cocoa powder, unsweetened
small pinch of kosher salt
3 cup half and half
1 tablespoon light corn syrup
4 ounces chopped bittersweet chocolate
2 tablespoons boiling water

Directions

1. Preheat oven to 375° F.
2. Coat your donut pan with cooking spray.
3. Mix all dry ingredients in a large mixing bowl. Whisk to blend well and aerate.
4. In a separate bowl, beat the eggs and stir in pumpkin and vanilla.
5. Gradually fold wet ingredients into dry ingredients until just combined.
6. Pipe batter into donut pan.
7. Bake for 7-8 minutes or until an inserted chopstick comes out clean.
8. Let cool directly in the pan.

For the frosting

1. Combine cocoa powder, sugar, salt, corn syrup and half and half over medium heat until boiling in a medium sauce pan. Pour over chopped chocolate and stir briskly with a spoon to dissolve chocolate. Stir in boiling water, a tablespoon at a time until the desired consistency is reached.
2. Spoon on cooled donuts into the frosting and decorate with desired toppings.

Buttermilk-Choco Donuts with Peanut Butter Glaze

Indulge yourself on this heavenly comfort food. It's good as a stress relief after a long and draining day or perfect for a nice and hot cup of coffee.

MAKES: 6 DONUTS
PREPARATION TIME: 5 minutes
BAKING TIME: 10 minutes

1 cup flour
¼ cup plus 2 tablespoons sugar
1 teaspoon baking powder
¼ cup cocoa powder
½ teaspoon salt
½ cup buttermilk
1 egg
½ teaspoon vanilla
1½ teaspoons melted butter

For the glaze:
2 tablespoons butter
¼ cup peanut butter
¼ cup powdered sugar
1 tablespoon milk

Directions

1. Preheat the oven to 325 °F.
2. Lightly grease a donut pan.
3. In a large bowl, whisk together all dry ingredients.
4. In a small bowl, whisk together the wet ingredients.
5. Add the wet ingredients to the dry ingredients and stir until well combined.
6. Spoon batter into the prepared pan.
7. Bake for 10 minutes or until cooked through.
8. Remove from the oven and cool in the pan for a few minutes.
9. Then transfer to a wire rack to cool further.

For the glaze

1. Heat the butter and peanut butter over low heat until smooth and melted using a small sauce pan. Remove from the heat and whisk in the milk and powdered sugar.
2. When the donuts are completely cool, dunk each in the glaze and return to wire rack to set.

Choco-Avocado Donuts

Avocadoes aren't just delicious and moist, but also loaded with essential nutrients. Each of these baked avocado donuts is high in protein, healthy fats and carbohydrates.

MAKES: 6 DONUTS
PREPARATION TIME: 20 minutes
BAKING TIME: 15 minutes

¼ ripe avocado
½ cup granulated sugar
1 egg
½ teaspoon vanilla extract
¼ cup all-purpose flour
¼ cup whole wheat flour
1/8 teaspoon baking soda
¾ teaspoons baking powder
¼ cup cocoa powder
1/8 teaspoon salt
6 tablespoons milk
½ cup powdered sugar

Directions

1. Preheat oven to 350°F.
2. Spray donut pan with nonstick spray.
3. In the bowl of a stand mixer, beat together the sugar and avocado until well combined.

4. Beat in the egg.
5. Stir in the vanilla.
6. In a small bowl, combine the white and wheat flour, baking powder, cocoa powder, baking soda and salt.
7. Slowly add the dry mixture to the avocado alternating with the milk, until everything is well incorporated.
8. Spoon the batter into the donut wells.
9. Bake for 12-15 minutes or until the donuts spring back when gently touched.
10. Cool completely before removing from the pan.
11. Toss in powdered sugar to coat.

Dark Chocolate and Pistachio Donuts

Imagine a luscious and smooth chocolate coating that starts to melt on your fingers as you take a bite of this gorgeous donut. Well don't just daydream on that. Go bake some of these goodies.

MAKES: 6 DONUTS
PREPARATION TIME: 5 minutes
BAKING TIME: 11 minutes

Cooking spray
2/3 cup unbleached all-purpose flour
½ teaspoon baking powder
¼ teaspoon baking soda
1/8 teaspoon salt
2/3 cup packed light brown sugar
½ cup vanilla bean Greek-style yogurt
1 large egg
1 teaspoon pure vanilla extract
½ bar dark chocolate, broken into pieces

Glaze:
½ bar dark chocolate, broken into pieces
2 tablespoons salted butter
¾ cup confectioners' sugar
about 2 tablespoons milk
2 tablespoons skinned pistachios, chopped

Directions

1. Preheat oven to 425°F.

2. Coat a 6-hole donut pan with cooking spray.
3. In small bowl, whisk together baking powder, flour, baking soda and the salt.
4. In another smaller bowl, also whisk together yogurt, brown sugar, egg and vanilla until no lumps of brown sugar remain.
5. Set third small heatproof bowl over small pan of just about simmering water; add chocolate and stir until melted.
6. Scrape melted chocolate into yogurt mixture and whisk until smooth.
7. Stir chocolate mixture into dry ingredients just until combined.
8. Spoon batter evenly into donut pan wells.
9. Bake for 9 to 11 minutes or until donuts feel set when lightly pressed.
10. Remove from oven and let stand in pan while you make glaze.

To make the glaze

1. In the bowl used to melt chocolate, combine chocolate and butter, return to pan of barely simmering water and stir until it melts. Remove bowl from heat and whisk in confectioners' sugar until well blended. Gradually whisk enough amount of milk to make smooth, thick, and glossy glaze.
2. Dip "well" side of each donut in glaze. Sprinkle each with pistachios.

Chocolate Chips and Oat Donuts

*Want a chocolate sweet treat without the starch of the regular flour?
This one's great for you. It's made out of oats, so you'll get the good old
fiber instead of carbs out on this.*

MAKES: 12 DONUTS
PREPARATION TIME: 5 minutes
BAKING TIME: 10 minutes

½ cup oats
1 egg
¼ cup unsweetened applesauce
¼ cup plain Greek yogurt
½ cup water
½ teaspoon vanilla extract
¾ teaspoon baking powder
¾ teaspoon baking soda
1/8 teaspoon salt
¼ teaspoon cream tartar
Your favorite sugar substitute equivalent to ½ cup of sugar
2 tablespoons chocolate chips

Directions

1. Preheat oven 350°F
2. Spray baking pan with non-stick cooking spray.
3. Blend all ingredients, except for chocolate chips,
   together in a blender or a food processor and blend

until mixture is smooth.

4. Spoon mixture into each donut cup.
5. Bake for 10 minutes. Poke with toothpick to make sure donuts are done.
6. Remove from oven and immediately add 5 chocolate chips to the tops of each donut.
7. Let the donuts cool completely before removing them from the pan or else they will break apart.

Quick Frosted German Donut

Whip up your homemade favorite in an instant. This recipe is a quick and easy way to satisfy your chocolate cravings. You'll get to enjoy your own donut in a little while.

MAKES: 12 DONUTS
PREPARATION TIME: 3 minutes
BAKING TIME: 13 minutes

1 box of German chocolate cake mix
1 cup almond milk
2 large eggs
1 stick of butter, melted
1 can of frosting, your choice
Toasted almond nuts, finely chopped

Directions

1. Preheat oven to 350°F.
2. Grease a donut pan.
3. Mix eggs, butter, milk and cake mix.
4. Stir until smooth.
5. Pour batter into donut pan up to ¾ full.
6. Bake for 11-13 minutes or until toothpick comes out clean after poking to the center of the donut.

7. Let them cool completely then transfer on a wire rack.

For the frosting

1. Put about half of the container of frosting in a microwavable bowl. Microwave for about 20 seconds and stir after. Repeat until frosting is melted enough for you to easily dip and coat the donuts.
2. Dip donuts upside down, put them back on cooling rack.
3. Sprinkle with almonds.

Mini Choco-Orange Zest Donuts

Give these baked chocolate-orange donuts a try. The sweetness of chocolate blends well with the tanginess of orange. You will surely love these baked mini goodies with your favorite drink.

MAKES: 12 MINI DONUTS
PREPARATION TIME: 5 minutes
BAKING TIME: 12 minutes

½ cup self-rising flour
¼ cup cocoa powder
4 tablespoons granulated sugar
1 teaspoon baking powder
6 tablespoons plain Greek yoghurt
4 tablespoons milk
½ teaspoon vanilla bean paste
¼ cup unsalted butter
1 egg
zest of an orange

For the glaze:
½ cups icing sugar
6 tablespoons orange juice
optional teaspoons orange zest to decorate

Directions

1. Preheat the oven to 170° C.
2. In a small mixing bowl sift all dry ingredients and mix together to incorporate.
3. In the bigger mixing bowl, whisk together the milk, yogurt, vanilla bean paste, butter, zest, and egg.
4. Combine two mixtures and make sure to incorporate everything well, but not to over-mix.
5. Transfer the batter into a piping bag with a large nozzle and pipe the mixture into your donut pans.
6. Bake for 10 - 12 minutes.
7. Leave the donuts to cool for about 10 minutes before you take them out the pan.
8. Before the donuts have cooled completely, use wooden spoon with a long handle and slot, then mount the donut onto it.
9. Dip it in the glaze and rotate it until the donut is completely covered.
10. Place on a wire rack and to let cool completely.
11. Feel free to decorate with a sprinkling of orange zest.

To make the glaze
1. In a shallow bowl, combine the icing sugar and the juice and mix together to form a smooth thin paste.
2. Add a drop tangerine gel paste to add a bit more color to glaze.

Choco-Peanut Butter Donut Balls

The melted candy corns, the peanut butter, and the chocolate glaze make these little fellas a triple treat in one tiny ball. It's a simple way to pamper your sweet tooth.

MAKES: 6 DONUTS
PREPARATION TIME: 7 minutes
BAKING TIME: 10 minutes

¼ cup candy corn
¼ cup peanut butter
¼ cup granulated sugar
1/3 cup plus 1 tablespoon milk
1 tablespoon canola oil
½ teaspoon vanilla extract
1 egg
1 cup all-purpose flour
1 teaspoon baking powder
¼ teaspoon salt

Chocolate Glaze:
2½ cups powdered sugar
2 tablespoons cocoa powder
½ teaspoon vanilla extract
4-5 tablespoons milk

Directions

1. Preheat oven to 325°F.
2. Lightly grease a cake pop pan.

3. Microwave candy corn in 30-second intervals until completely melted.
4. Add peanut butter and stir until smooth. Microwave it again if necessary.
5. Transfer candy corn mixture into a medium-sized bowl.
6. Stir in sugar until completely combined.
7. Add vanilla extract, canola oil, milk, and egg.
8. Fold in flour, salt, and baking powder, stirring until just combined.
9. Place batter in a piping bag.
10. Fill cake pop pan cavities 2/3 full.
11. Bake for 8-10 minutes or until a toothpick inserted in center comes out clean.
12. Let them cool a bit in the pan before moving them to a wire rack and allow it to cool completely before glazing.

For the glaze

1. Combine all ingredients together. Gradually add more milk to reach desired consistency.
2. Dip each donut hole into the glaze then place them in small muffin cups to make sure they won't stick with each other and for a nicer presentation.

Double Trouble Mini Chocolate Donuts

This donut is a good one. With buttermilk and eggs in the dough;
chocolate frosting; plus chocolate chips on top, it's a perfect treat.

MAKES: 24 MINI DONUTS
PREPARATION TIME: 5 minutes
BAKING TIME: 9 minutes

2 cups cake flour
1 cup sugar
2½ tablespoons cocoa powder
1½ teaspoon baking powder
pinch of salt
2 tablespoons sour cream
2 eggs
1 cup buttermilk

Chocolate glaze:
2 cups powdered sugar
2 tablespoons cocoa powder
¼ cup whole milk or more if necessary
½ teaspoon vanilla extract

Directions

1. Preheat oven to 350°F.
2. Lightly grease 24-count mini donut pan.
3. In a bowl, whisk together the cake flour, cocoa powder, baking powder, sugar and salt.
4. Add the sour cream, buttermilk, and eggs just until combined.
5. Spoon the batter equally into your donut pan. Fill them at ¾ full each to give room for expansion.
6. Bake for 9 minutes or until an inserted toothpick comes out clean.
7. Let donuts cool in the pan for a while then remove them to cool on a wire rack.

For the glaze

1. In a small bowl, mix together the powdered sugar, milk, cocoa powder and vanilla. Whisk until combined and have a nice thick glaze.
2. Dip the donuts into the glaze and place back on wire rack to set.
3. You may add sprinkles.

Gluten-Free Choc-o-nuts

Gluten-free Cho-o-nuts is far from being boring. This sweet and lemony chocolate donut is quite satisfying to the taste buds.

MAKES: 12 DONUTS
PREPARATION TIME: 15 minutes
BAKING TIME: 10 minutes

¾ cup gluten-free oat flour
¼ cup potato starch or arrowroot powder
½ cup granulated sugar
¼ teaspoon xanthan gum
¼ cup cocoa powder
½ teaspoon gluten-free baking soda
½ teaspoon vanilla extract
1 large egg
6 tablespoons sour cream
¼ cup milk
¼ cup vegetable oil
nonstick cooking spray

For the Glaze:
1½ cups powdered sugar
6 tablespoons whole milk
½ teaspoon lemon extract
1 teaspoon vanilla extract

Directions

1. Preheat oven to 350°F.
2. Combine and whisk together oat flour, potato starch, granulated sugar, xanthan gum, cocoa powder, and baking soda in a medium bowl. Add egg, sour cream, vegetable oil, and milk. Whisk until batter is smooth. Let stand for five minutes.
3. Lightly coat pan with nonstick cooking spray.
4. Fill holes about halfway with batter.
5. Bake for 10 minutes or until donuts spring back to the touch.
6. Turn donuts out onto a wire rack to cool.

For glaze

1. Whisk together vanilla, powdered sugar, milk and lemon extract in small bowl.
2. Dip donuts, one at a time, into glaze and shake off excess. Place dipped donuts back to wire rack. Store donuts covered at room temperature for up to three days.

Vegan Mixed Medley Donuts

*Being a vegan pastry, these donuts are great! But in addition to that,
these are also low in fat and won't need donut pans to bake; a regular
baking pan can also do it.*

MAKES: 12 DONUTS
PREPARATION TIME: 25 minutes
BAKING TIME: 15 minutes

*1⅓ cups pure cane sugar
1 cup pure sweet potato puree
1 cup unsweetened almond milk
5 tablespoons melted virgin coconut oil
1 teaspoon vanilla extract
1 teaspoon pure almond extract
3 cups all-purpose flour
2/3 cup cocoa powder
4 teaspoons gluten-free baking powder
½ teaspoon salt*

For the Glazing:
*2 cups vegan chocolate chips
¼ cup virgin coconut oil
sliced almonds, lightly toasted*

Directions

1. Preheat the oven to 350ºF.
2. Line a baking tray with parchment paper.
3. In a large mixing bowl, whisk the sugar, sweet potato puree, almond milk, coconut oil, vanilla and almond extracts together.
4. In a separate bowl, sift flour, baking powder, cocoa powder, and salt and then stir this into the wet mixture until evenly blended. Cover and let it set for 15 minutes.
5. Turn the dough out onto a lightly floured work surface and roll out to ¾-inch thickness. Cut out dough with a 3-inch dough cutter, the remaining dough can be baked as donut holes. Place the donuts onto the prepared baking tray and bake for 15 minutes. Cool the donuts completely.

For the glaze

1. Melt the chocolate chips and coconut oil together in a metal bowl placed over a pot of gently simmering water, stirring until it completely melts.
2. Let the chocolate melt until it has thickened to a glaze consistency. Dip the donuts in and return to the tray.
3. Sprinkle with sliced almonds and let the glaze set for 30 minutes.
4. Donuts are best enjoyed on the day they are baked.

Fruity Chocolate Donuts

Treat your senses with a sweet chocolate glazed donut. Adding fresh fruits on top makes the whole experience refreshing and healthier.

MAKES: 6 DONUTS
PREPARATION TIME: 5 minutes
BAKING TIME: 10 minutes

---

2 tablespoons superfine sugar
½ cup warm soymilk
½ tablespoon active dry yeast
A pinch of salt
1 teaspoon vanilla extract
½ cup cake flour
1¼ cups all-purpose flour
3 tablespoons cold butter

Topping:
2 tablespoons cocoa powder, unsweetened
2 tablespoons powdered sugar
3 tablespoons water
1 square of non-dairy cooking chocolate

Directions

1. Preheat oven to 400°F.
2. In a food processor, put the milk, yeast, salt, sugar,

and vanilla in the processor bowl and pulse to mix well.

3. Add the cake flour and 1 cup of all-purpose flour then process, adding a little more of the flour as necessary till the dough is thick and pulls away from the sides of the bowl.

4. Now add the butter.

5. Add the rest of the flour until you have soft and elastic dough that is moist but not overly sticky to touch.

6. Turn the dough out onto a floured surface and knead gently until the dough no longer sticks to hands.

7. Shape the dough into a ball and place in a lightly greased large mixing bowl turning it around to coat well.

8. Cover with a damp towel and let it rise for about an hour or until double in volume.

9. Push down the dough and roll out to 1/2-inch thick.

10. Cut out donuts using a donut cutter to cut out 3" diameter with 1-inch diameter holes. Do not twist the cutter or else you will end up with multi circles.

11. Remove excess dough and re-roll then cut out more donuts.

12. Place the donuts on lightly greased baking sheets leaving at least 1-inch space between each of them. Let them rise for about 20 minutes or until almost double in size.

13. Bake for about 5 to 10 minutes until they're done and golden browned. Make sure not to over bake.

For chocolate glaze

1. Combine all ingredients. Melt on slow flame until it becomes saucy and coats the spoon. You may also sprinkle it with water if required or if the sauce is too thick.

2. Dip the tops of donuts while the glaze is still warm.

3. Top them with sliced fruits of your choice.

4. Invert and set aside to set.

Brown Chocolate Glaze Donuts

Now is the perfect time to take out that donut pan again. These buttery glazed donuts are paired with chocolate which makes them a perfect fit.

MAKES: 12 DONUTS
PREPARATION TIME: 10 minutes
BAKING TIME: 10 minutes

1 cup all-purpose flour
¾ teaspoon baking powder
¼ teaspoon baking soda
½ teaspoon salt
½ teaspoon freshly grated nutmeg
1/3 cup granulated sugar
3 tablespoons unsalted butter
1 large egg
½ cup buttermilk
1 teaspoon pure vanilla extract

For the Chocolate Glaze
1½ cups powdered sugar
4 tablespoons cocoa powder, unsweetened
pinch of salt
3 to 4 tablespoons milk
1 teaspoon pure vanilla extract

Directions

1. Place a rack in the upper third of the oven and preheat oven to 350° F.
2. Lightly grease a donut pan.
3. In a medium bowl, mix all dry ingredients.
4. In a small saucepan, melt butter over medium-low heat. Remove it from heat and immediately transfer browned butter to a small bowl quickly after it turns medium brown.
5. In another small bowl whisk together 3 remaining wet ingredients.
6. Measure out 2 tablespoons of browned butter and whisk into the wet ingredients mixture.
7. Add the wet ingredients all at once to the dry ingredients and stir together until no flour lumps remain and all of the ingredients are well combined.
8. Use a small spoon to place the batter into the prepared pan. Smooth out and fill each well in the pan three-quarters full with batter.
9. Bake for 8 to 10 minutes. Keep an eye on them and try not to over-bake them.
10. Remove the pan from the oven and allow it to cool in before inverting onto a wire rack to cool completely.

To make the glaze

1. In a medium bowl, whisk together sugar, cocoa powder, and salt. Add 2 tablespoons of milk and vanilla extract. Whisk all to combine. Add more milk as needed to create a thick but still pourable glaze.
2. Once the donuts are completely cooled, dip top-side-down into the chocolate glaze.
3. Return to the wire rack and sprinkle with toppings.
4. Allow to set for about 30 minutes.

Chocolate Overload Mini Donuts

Even just by the sound of chocolate overload is mouthwatering. With chocolate from bottom to top, and from core to cover, these little buddies are a temptation with a hole!

MAKES: 24 MINI DONUTS
PREPARATION TIME: 5 minutes
BAKING TIME: 14 minutes

½ cup oat flour, gluten free
½ cup sweet rice flour
2 tablespoons coconut flour
¼ cup unsweetened cocoa powder
½ cup pure cane sugar
1 teaspoon espresso powder
½ teaspoon Celtic sea salt
1 teaspoon baking powder
3 tablespoons coconut oil
2 large eggs, lightly beaten
¾ cup buttermilk
3 tablespoons organic, unsweetened apple sauce
1 teaspoon vanilla
½ cup of mini bittersweet chocolate chips
3 tablespoons shredded coconut

For the glaze
2 tablespoons butter, unsalted and at room temperature
2 tablespoons honey
1 cup bittersweet chocolate, chopped fine
1 teaspoon pure vanilla extract

2 cups powdered sugar

***

Directions

1. Preheat your oven to 350°F.
2. Line a rimmed baking sheet with parchment.
3. Grease your mini donut pans with a bit of shortening and place on the parchment lined baking sheet.
4. In a large bowl, whisk all of the dry ingredients.
5. Make a well in the center of the dry ingredients.
6. Using a rubber spatula, fold in the eggs, buttermilk, coconut oil, and vanilla.
7. Add the applesauce and mix to combine.
8. Fold in the chocolate chips.
9. Fill batter in a pastry bag fitted with a plain round tip.
10. Pipe batter into prepared donut pans filling up ¾ full.
11. Bake for 14 minutes.
12. Rotating pans front to back, at the half way through baking.
13. Cool donuts on wire racks when done.
14. While donuts cool to room temperature, go toast the coconut.

For the glaze

1. Place a glass bowl over a small pan of simmering water. Place butter, honey, and bittersweet chocolate in the glass bowl until all is melted and combined. Remove glass bowl from the sauce pan and off heat, add vanilla. Then let sit to room temperature.
2. Dip each donut into glaze.
3. Place back on a wire rack and garnish with toasted coconut.
4. Place donuts in the fridge for about 30 minutes to set the glaze.

SHADES OF FRUITS AND VEGGIE DONUTS

Strawberry Ganache Cake Donuts

With homemade white chocolate ganache and fresh strawberry compote, these donuts have their perfect match. Enjoy a truly delectable taste in every single bite.

MAKES: 6 DONUTS
PREPARATION TIME: 30 minutes
BAKING TIME: 8 minutes

---

1 egg
½ cup milk
4 tablespoons butter, melted
¾ cup strawberry compote
1 teaspoon vanilla

1½ cup all-purpose flour
½ cup sugar
1½ teaspoons baking powder
½ teaspoon. baking soda
½ teaspoon salt

Strawberry Compote:
1 cup hulled and diced fresh strawberries
¼ cup sugar

White Chocolate Ganache:
1¼ cup white chocolate chips
½ cup heavy cream
1 tablespoons corn syrup

Directions

For the compote:
1. In a saucepan, over medium heat, add strawberries and sugar then stir occasionally.
2. After 10 minutes, start mashing the strawberries with spoon.
3. The compote will have some small pieces, if you don't want them you may strain them out. The whole process may take about 18 minutes.
4. After the compote has come to the perfect consistency, take it off the heat and let it cool for about 5 minutes.

Donut:
1. Preheat the oven to 425°F.
2. Spray the donut pan with non-stick cooking spray.
3. In a large bowl, add the egg and milk, and whisk them until blended.
4. Add the strawberry compote, butter, and vanilla. Whisk until everything is well combined.
5. In a separate bowl, mix the flour, the baking powder,

baking soda, salt, and also the sugar.

6. Once all the dry ingredients are combined, make a well in the middle then add a small amount of the wet mixture and whisk. Keep doing this until all the batter is done.

7. Scoop the batter into a disposable piping bag and snip a small hole in one the tip.

8. Fill the bottom of the pan with the batter, filling half full only.

9. Bake in the oven for 8 minutes or until they're done. Observe it until the bottoms are golden brown and the tops are pale pink.

10. Remove pan from oven and let cool for at least 5 minutes.

11. Place the donuts onto the cooling rack to cool further.

For the Ganache:

1. In a microwavable bowl, add corn syrup, heavy cream and white chocolate. Heat it into the microwave for 45 seconds. Take the bowl out and whisk until everything is well combined. Let it cool for about 10 minutes until ganache has thickened.

2. Dip the cooled donuts one by one into the ganache and place them back onto the cooling rack.

3. You may add slices of strawberries on top.

Go-Shrek Donuts

Try this wheat donut glazed with Shrek's color from the combination of spinach and sugar. You will surely have a healthy and fulfilling treat in every bite.

MAKES: 6 DONUTS
PREPARATION TIME: 5 minutes
BAKING TIME: 10 minutes

½ cup whole wheat pastry flour
½ cup all-purpose flour
¼ cup sugar
¾ teaspoon baking powder
¼ teaspoon salt
1/3 cup buttermilk
1 egg
1/8 cup honey
1 tablespoon butter, melted
1 tablespoon vanilla

Green Glaze:
½ cup powdered sugar
2 tablespoons fresh spinach juice

Directions

1. Preheat oven to 400°F.
2. Lightly coat a donut pan with cooking spray.
3. Combine dry ingredients in a bowl and stir well using a whisk.
4. In a second bowl, combine egg, buttermilk, honey, butter, and vanilla, stirring well using a whisk.
5. Add liquid mixture to flour mixture and mix until just combined.
6. Pipe the batter into the pan using a large plastic bag with a corner cut off.
7. Bake for 8-10 minutes or until donuts turn slightly golden at the bottom.
8. Cool in pan about 5 minutes.
9. Remove donuts from pan and let them cool completely on a wire rack.

Make the glaze

1. Mix sugar and juice together until thick and smooth. Add more liquid or sugar as needed to get the right consistency.
2. Spread it over cooled donuts.

Oat Cherry Glazed Donuts

Treat your kids on the weekend with these pretty donuts. The sweetness of fresh cherries in this glaze makes them extra special and tasty.

MAKES: 6 DONUTS
PREPARATION TIME: 10 minutes
BAKING TIME: 13 minutes

¾ cup unbleached all-purpose flour
½ cup whole wheat pastry flour
¼ cup oat flour
1½ teaspoons baking powder
¼ teaspoon salt
pinch cinnamon
pinch nutmeg, optional
½ cup pure cherry juice
¼ cup almond
½ cup unrefined sugar
2 tablespoons melted coconut butter
1 teaspoon vanilla extract
3-4 tablespoons pitted and very finely chopped fresh sweet cherries

For Cherry Glaze:
½ cup organic powdered sugar
1-2 tablespoons pure cherry juice
¼ teaspoon vanilla extract

Directions

1. Preheat oven to 350 degrees.
2. Lightly grease a 6-count donut pan with coconut oil.
3. In a large bowl, whisk together flours, cinnamon, salt, nutmeg, and baking powder.
4. In a glass measuring cup, mix coconut butter, sugar, vanilla extract, cherry juice, and almond milk all together.
5. Add the mixture of wet ingredients to the dry ingredients mixture and whisk until no more lumps remain. Gradually fold in chopped cherries.
6. Spoon batter evenly into pan.
7. Bake for 11-13 minutes or until donuts looks golden on top. Take out pan from oven and allow donuts to cool in the pan for at least 5 minutes before placing them onto a cooling rack.

For the glaze

1. In a shallow bowl, whisk together cherry juice, powdered sugar, and vanilla extract. Gradually pour the cherry juice until you reach the consistency you want.
2. Once donuts are cooled, dip the top half of each donut in the glaze and allow them to dry.

Blueberry Donut with Lemon Glaze

The fresh blueberries in this dough give tender flavor and texture. Plus the lemon zest and rind on top add even more delight.

MAKES: 12 DONUTS
PREPARATION TIME: 25 minutes
BAKING TIME: 12 minutes

1½ cups gluten-free flour of your choice
2 large eggs
¾ cup granulated sugar
1 cup wild blueberries, rinsed and pat dried
1 cup sour cream
zest of 1 lemon
2 tablespoons lemon juice
2 tablespoons melted butter
1 tablespoon oil
1 teaspoon vanilla extract
1 teaspoon baking powder
½ teaspoon gluten-free baking soda
pinch of salt

For the glaze:
2 tablespoons butter
¼ cup lemon juice
grated lemon rind
2½ cups powdered sugar, plus more for dusting

Directions

1. Preheat oven to 325 °F
2. Grease a 12-cavity donut pan with spray or butter.
3. In the bowl of a standing mixer fitted with balloon whisk, whip sugar and eggs on medium-high for 3 minutes until fluffy. Add sour cream, lemon zest, and lemon juice and stir to combine all.
4. In a small bowl, mix butter, oil and vanilla, and add this to egg mixture. Stir well to combine.
5. In a medium bowl, whisk together the baking powder, flour, salt, and baking soda. Add berries in and toss gently using a fork to coat.
6. Add berry mixture to wet ingredients. Stir gently with a wooden spoon folding in the berries until combined.
7. Place half of the batter in a pastry bag. Cut a ½-inch hole at one tip of the bag. Pipe batter into the cavities of the donut pan about 2/3 full.
8. Bake donuts on middle rack of oven for 12 minutes. Cool for 5 minutes then remove from pan. Repeat procedure for remaining batter.
9. Allow donuts to cool on a wire rack.

For the glaze

1. Melt butter in a small bowl. Whisk in lemon juice and powdered sugar until smooth. Transfer to a smaller but wider bowl to freely dip in donut.
2. Dip the bottom of each donut in the glaze then place on a wire rack to set. When all donuts have been glazed and glaze has set, dust them with powdered sugar then sprinkle with some grated lemon rind.

Baked Coco-Mango Donuts

The sweet smelling and luscious tasting mango fruit gives double dose of delightfulness to donuts. You will know it's a delicious even just by the smell of it!

MAKES: 6 DONUTS
PREPARATION TIME: 10 minutes
BAKING TIME: 15 minutes

½ cup coconut oil, melted
2/3 cup brown sugar
¼ cup coconut oil
¾ cup coconut milk
1 teaspoon white vinegar
1 teaspoon vanilla
2 cups all-purpose flour
2 teaspoon baking powder
1 teaspoon baking soda
½ teaspoon salt
½ cup shredded coconut
½ cup diced mango

Glaze:
1½ cups powdered sugar
2 tablespoons coconut milk
1 cup shredded coconut, toasted

Directions

1. Preheat oven to 375°F
2. Combine the flour, baking powder, baking soda, shredded coconut, and salt in a large bowl. Combine the coconut milk, vinegar and vanilla in a measuring glass. Beat together the coconut oil, sugar and the oil.
3. Combine the flour mixture and the coconut milk mixture, alternating it and always ending on dry ingredients mixture. Once combined, mix in the mango.
4. Put the batter into a large pastry bag and push it down into one corner, trim off about half an inch of the corner and pipe the batter into the greased donut pan.
5. Bake 15 minutes or until golden brown and springy when you touch it.

For the glaze

1. Put the powdered sugar in a bowl and slowly add in coconut milk until desired consistency is acquired. You may dip the tail end of a wooden spoon in the glaze and allow excess to drip off, this allows you to see how opaque the mixture is and you may add milk or sugar if needed.
2. Remove donuts from the pan and let them cool at least partially. Dip each in glaze, then in toasted coconut and place them in a rack to dry.

Cinnapple Donuts

Preparation Time: 15 Minutes
Baking Time: 15-18 Minutes
Makes: 6 Donuts

---

3 tablespoons Light Brown Sugar
3 tablespoons White Sugar
1 cup (about 1½ apples) coarsely grated Apple, skin removed and cored
1 cups All-Purpose White Flour
1¼ teaspoon Baking Powder
¼ teaspoon Salt
2/3 teaspoon grated Nutmeg
4 tablespoons Butter, cold and cut into small pieces
1 large Egg
3 tablespoons Milk (add a little more if the batter appears too dry)

Topping Ingredients:
3 tablespoons melted Unsalted Butter
3 tablespoons White Sugar
1 teaspoon Cinnamon Powder

Directions

1. Preheat your oven to 350 degrees Fahrenheit. Prepare a 6-cavity donut pan by greasing it. In a bowl, combine the flour, light brown sugar, white sugar, baking powder, nutmeg and salt. Add in the butter, and mix it with the previous flour mixture until it looks like bread crumbs. Place aside.

2. In a different bowl, whisk the egg. Add in the milk and mix in the apples. Combine the egg mixture with the flour mixture. Mix together using a baking spoon or

spatula while ensuring that you do not over-mix the mixture. Put about two spoons of the batter into prepared donut pan.

3. Allow to bake for approximately 15-18 minutes or until the donuts are golden in color. Cool for up to 5 minutes. Remove each donut gently and then lightly brush each donut with the melted unsalted butter. Dip each donut in a bowl with the white sugar and cinnamon powder already combined. Shake donuts to remove any excess sugar before serving.

Carrot Cake Donut

Enjoy the all-time-favorite carrot cake in every bite of these frosted carrot cake donut packed with nutrients from the combination of its ingredients.

MAKES: 6 DONUTS
PREPARATION TIME: 10 minutes
BAKING TIME: 10 minutes

1/3 cup whole wheat flour
1/3 cup all-purpose flour
3 tablespoons brown sugar
2/3 teaspoon baking powder
pinch salt
½ teaspoon cinnamon
pinch nutmeg
pinch allspice
1 tablespoon butter, melted and cooled
1 egg
1/3 cup non-fat milk
1/3 teaspoon vanilla extract
1/3 cup shredded carrots

For the Frosting:
1/3 of low fat cream cheese
¾ teaspoon butter, softened
1½ tablespoons confectioner's sugar

1/3 teaspoon vanilla extract
Pinch salt
Carrot, coarsely grated-for topping

Directions

1. Preheat oven to 350°F.
2. Lightly spray donut pan with non-stick cooking spray.
3. In a large bowl, whisk together all dry ingredients, except for the carrots, until well-combined.
4. In a small bowl, whisk together all wet ingredients.
5. Add wet ingredients to dry ingredients and stir until just combined.
6. Stir in shredded carrots.
7. Pour batter into a pastry bag or with one corner cut off.
8. Fill donut cavity about ½ full.
9. Bake for 8-10 minutes.
10. Allow donuts to cool for 2 minutes before removing from pan to a wire rack to cool completely.
11. While donuts are cooling, start preparing the frosting.

For the frosting

1. Beat together cream cheese and butter until turn smooth and creamy. Next, add confectioner's sugar, vanilla extract, and salt. Beat until it's smooth.
2. Spread frosting over the top and sprinkle with carrot bits of cooled donuts.
3. Let the frosting set for a while.

Pumpkin-Glazed Flax Donuts

It's good to have pumpkin in the dough, but to have it in the glaze is even better. Why not! It's a new way to enjoy the good old donuts.

MAKES: 6 DONUTS
PREPARATION TIME: 10 minutes
BAKING TIME: 9 minutes

1 cup all-purpose flour
5 tablespoons granulated sugar
1 teaspoon baking powder
½ teaspoon salt
pinch nutmeg
pinch cinnamon
6 tablespoons soymilk
½ teaspoon apple cider vinegar
1 tablespoon ground flax seeds
6 tablespoons warm water
1 tablespoon vegan butter or almond butter

Glaze:
1 cup powdered sugar
2 tablespoons of your almond milk
1½ teaspoons ground cinnamon
5 teaspoons pumpkin puree

Directions

1. Preheat oven to 425°F.
2. Grease or spray donut pan.
3. In a measuring cup, combine soymilk and apple cider vinegar and set aside for 5 minutes.
4. In a large bowl, combine, baking powder, salt, flour, sugar, cinnamon, and nutmeg.
5. In a smaller bowl, whisk together the flax seeds and 4 tablespoons warm water.
6. Whisk flax mixture, vegan butter, and soymilk mixture into the dry ingredients until just combined.
7. Fill each donut cavity with batter until 2/3 full.
8. Bake 8-9 minutes or until donuts turn golden brown.
9. Allow pan to cool about 5 minutes before removing donuts and place on wire rack.

For the glaze

1. Whisk together all the ingredients until they thoroughly combine. If needed, add more milk to make the glaze thinner, or more powdered sugar to thicken.
2. Dip donuts in for a solid layer of glaze.

Orange Blues Donuts

These fruity and fluffy baked donuts are glazed with the perfect combination of blueberry and orange. These donuts have an inviting aroma that will surely tempt everyone around.

MAKES: 12 DONUTS
PREPARATION TIME: 10 minutes
BAKING TIME: 16 minutes

¾ cup all-purpose flour
5 tablespoons superfine sugar (or caster sugar)
½ teaspoon baking powder
¼ teaspoon baking soda
1/8 teaspoon salt
1 egg
½ cup nonfat Greek yogurt
2 tablespoons milk
2 tablespoons all natural apple sauce
¼ teaspoon vanilla extract
zest of half an orange
½ cups fresh blueberries

For the Blueberry Glaze:
¼ cup fresh blueberries
juice of ¼ orange
1 cup powdered sugar, sifted

Directions

1. Preheat oven to 350°F.
2. In a mixing bowl combine all dry ingredients except for the blueberries. Whisk thoroughly to eliminate lumps and set aside.
3. In a separate mixing bowl combine the wet ingredients and whisk together.
4. Pour the wet mixture into the dry mixture and stir together.
5. Carefully fold in blueberries until just combined and thick.
6. Scoop batter into a piping bag and snip the tip.
7. Pipe batter into greased donut pans and bake for 12-16 minutes or until slightly darker than golden brown.
8. Remove from oven and allow donuts to sit in the pan for 5 minutes.
9. Carefully remove them from pan and place onto a cooling rack to cool completely.
10. Fully dip each donut into the glaze and gently tap to remove excess.
11. Return glazed donuts on to the cooling rack, and allow glaze to set for about 10 minutes.

To make the glaze

1. Put blueberries into a food processor and puree until smooth.
2. Add the orange juice and powdered sugar, half a cup at each time, until fully incorporated and no lumps remain.

Double Orange Donuts

Delight yourself on the tanginess of these orange donuts from the inside out. Orange flavored donuts glazed with the blend of orange and the sweetness of sugar.

MAKES: 6 DONUTS
PREPARATION TIME: 30 minutes
BAKING TIME: 12 minutes

---

3 tablespoons butter, softened
5 tablespoons brown sugar
5 tablespoons granulated sugar
¾ teaspoon vanilla extract
1 egg
4 tablespoons vanilla yogurt
5 tablespoons orange juice
¾ teaspoon baking powder
¾ teaspoon baking soda
1¼ cups flour
¼ teaspoon salt
½ teaspoon cinnamon
½ cup orange pieces

For the Glaze:
1 cup powdered sugar
1/8 cup orange juice
1/8 cup white sanding sugar (this is a kind of decorating sugar which can be substituted with regular sugar)

Directions

1. Preheat oven at 375°F.
2. Lightly grease donut pan.
3. In a large mixing bowl, cream the sugars and butter.
4. Add the egg, yogurt, and vanilla and mix until smooth and creamy.
5. Sift dry ingredients all together.
6. Gradually add to the butter mixture alternately with the orange juice. But do not over mix.
7. Stir in the orange pieces.
8. Spoon batter into a piping bag then snip the tip with a hole that is big enough for orange pieces to pass through.
9. Pipe the batter into the pan wells about 2/3 full.
10. Bake for 12 minutes.
11. Remove from oven and cool donuts in there for 3 minutes.
12. Gently transfer them on a wire rack to cool completely.
13. Stir together powdered sugar and orange juice.
14. Dip the tops of cooled donuts in the glaze then sprinkle with the sanding sugar.
15. Let them set completely.

Raised Mango Pistachio Donuts

This donut is softer and lighter than cake donuts. This unusual combination of mango and pistachio give these donuts a fruity and nutty flavor.

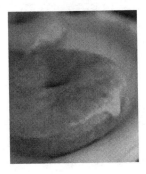

MAKES: 12 DONUTS
PREPARATION TIME: 1 hour and 45 minutes
BAKING TIME: 8 minutes

---

1 egg
¼ cup superfine sugar
1 cup whole milk, heated to 115 degrees
1 tablespoon active dry yeast
1 teaspoon salt
2 teaspoons vanilla extract
2½ to 3½ cups all-purpose flour, separated, plus extra for kneading
½ cup butter, cut into 1-inch cubes

For the Glaze:
¼ cup mango pulp
1½ cups of icing sugar
1/3 cup of shelled and finely chopped unsalted pistachios

Directions

1. In the bowl of a stand mixer fitted with the paddle attachment, beat sugar and egg on medium speed for about a minute until blended. Add the yeast, salt, milk, and vanilla, and again stir to blend. Adjust the machine on low speed then add 2 cups of flour, about half a cup at a time, and beat until the dough is thick enough and pulls away from the sides of the bowl.

2. Now with the machine on medium speed, add the butter cubes one piece at a time, and beat for 5 minutes until no large chunks of butter remain. Reduce speed to low and gradually add additional flour until the dough collects around the hook and cleans the sides of the bowl. It will be soft and moist, but not too sticky.

3. Switch to the hook. Place the dough out onto a floured surface and knead gently until the dough no longer sticks on your hands.

4. Transfer the dough to a lightly greased large bowl and turn to coat. Cover it with a damp tea towel and let rise in a warm space for an hour until volume doubles.

5. Punch the dough down and roll out to ½ -inch thick. Using a donut cutter, cut out 3-inch-diameter rounds with l-inch-diameter holes.

6. Cut out holes can also be baked as donut holes.

7. Preheat the oven to 400°F. Line a baking sheet with parchment paper.

8. Place the donuts at least 1 inch apart on the baking sheet to give space for expansion. Cover with cling wrap and let sit in a warm space for 20 minutes until nearly doubled in size.

9. Bake for 5 to 8 minutes until the donuts turn to light golden brown; being very careful not to over bake them.

For the glaze

1. In another small bowl mix the icing sugar and mango pulp until well combined, then set the glaze aside.
2. Dip the freshly baked donuts in the glaze and place them on a plate.
3. Immediately sprinkle the finely chopped pistachios over the top and allow it to set for a time.

Glazed Blackberry Donuts

Enjoy whole blackberries in every bite of this delectable pureed blackberry glazed baked donuts. You will surely reap the antioxidant goodness that is stored in the blackberries from this piece of treat.

MAKES: 6 DONUTS
PREPARATION TIME: 20 minutes
BAKING TIME: 17 minutes

¾ cups all-purpose flour
5 tablespoons superfine sugar (or caster sugar)
¾ teaspoon ground cardamom
½ teaspoon baking powder
¼ teaspoon baking soda
¼ teaspoon salt
1 egg
½ cup nonfat Greek yogurt
1½ tablespoons milk
1½ tablespoons all-natural apple sauce
¼ teaspoon vanilla extract
zest of ½ lemon
¾ cups fresh blackberries

Blackberry glaze:
1 cup fresh blackberries
juice of ¼ lemon
¾ teaspoon vanilla extract
2 cups powdered sugar

Directions

1. Preheat oven to 350°F.
2. In a mixing bowl, sift dry ingredients all together, except for the berries.
3. In another mixing bowl, add wet ingredients and whisk together.
4. Add the wet mixture to the dry mixture and stir together.
5. Gently fold in the blackberries until just combined and thickened.
6. Scoop batter into a re-closable plastic bag and snip the tip with a hole enough for berries to pass through.
7. Pipe the batter into greased pan.
8. Bake for 15 to 17 minutes or until slightly darker than golden brown.
9. Remove from oven and allow donuts to sit for 5 minutes.
10. Remove from molds and place onto a cooling rack to let cool completely.
11. Fully dip each donut into blackberry glaze and tap to remove excess.
12. Allow glazed donuts to set for about 20 minutes.

To make the blackberry glaze

1. Place blackberries into a food processor and puree until smooth.
2. Strain.
3. Add vanilla and powdered sugar, ½ cup at each time, and whisk until no lumps remain.

Donuts with Lemony Blackberry Sauce

You don't have to have a hard time on deciding whether to have blackberry or lemon flavored donut. Why bother making it hard when you can enjoy both in one mouth-watering delight!

MAKES: 12 DONUTS
PREPARATION TIME: 20 minutes
BAKING TIME: 9 minutes

1¾ cups all-purpose flour
½ cup lemon yogurt
¾ cup milk
¾ cup sugar
2 eggs, lightly beaten
2 tablespoons butter, melted
2 teaspoon baking powder
¾ teaspoon salt
½ teaspoon vanilla

For Blackberry Sauce:
1 cup blackberries
½ cup sugar
1 tablespoon lemon juice

For the Glaze:
1 cup powdered sugar
½ teaspoon lemon juice (or to taste)
About 1/8 cup water (or use enough to get your desired consistency)

Directions

1. Preheat oven to 425°F.
2. Spray donut pan with cooking spray.
3. In a stand mixer, whisk flour, baking powder, sugar, and salt all together.
4. Beat in lemon yogurt, vanilla, eggs, milk and melted butter until fully incorporated.
5. Pipe the batter into each pan well about half-full.
6. Spoon two to three teaspoon of blackberry sauce on top of the batter.
7. Using a wooden skewer, swirl the sauce into the donut batter.
8. Bake in oven for 9 minutes.
9. Remove from oven, cool for five minutes then transfer on a cooling rack.
10. Once they cooled completely, dip each donut top into glaze to cover.
11. Place back on the rack for glaze to set.

To make the Sauce

1. In small saucepan over medium-high heat, fold blackberries, sugar and lemon juice.
2. Mash blackberries with a fork.
3. Continue to stir until boiling.
4. Remove from heat and pour through a strain to remove all seeds.
5. Set it aside to cool and thicken.

To make the glaze

1. In small bowl, whisk powdered sugar with enough lemon juice to taste and also enough water to get the desired consistency.

Nutty Carrot-Pineapple Donut

These are heavenly homemade donuts packed with the perfect combination of pineapple and carrots. You will surely love these sweet-smelling donuts with a nutty blend from walnuts.

MAKES: 10 DONUTS
PREPARATION TIME: 5 minutes
BAKING TIME: 10 minutes

---

5 tablespoons butter, softened
1 egg
1/8 teaspoon salt
1/8 teaspoon vanilla
½ cup brown sugar
½ cup vanilla yogurt
½ cup crushed pineapple, drained (reserve juice)
½ cup shredded carrots
½ teaspoons cinnamon
1/8 teaspoon nutmeg
½ teaspoons baking powder
½ teaspoons baking soda
1 cup flour

Frosting:
3 tablespoons cream cheese
1 tablespoon butter
1 tablespoons pineapple juice
1/3 cup powdered sugar
¼ cup chopped walnuts

Directions

2. Preheat oven to 375°F.
3. In a large bowl, beat the sugar and butter with a hand mixer.
4. Add the yogurt, egg, and vanilla into the bowl.
5. Add the pineapple and carrots.
6. Mix everything thoroughly.
7. Use a medium bowl to combine the cinnamon, baking soda, baking powder, flour, salt, and nutmeg using a metal wire whisk.
8. Combine the two mixtures.
9. Sift the dry ingredients into the mixture. For best results and easier stirring, sift small amounts at a time between stirring.
10. Grease 6-count pan.
11. Fill a donut pan. Add the batter to the cavities of the pan, up to about ½ full.
12. Bake the donuts for 10 minutes.
13. Allow the donuts to cool. Leave them in the pan for a few minutes.
14. Transfer the donuts to a wire cooling rack for about 15 to 20 minutes.

For the frosting

1. Combine the frosting ingredients together, except the walnuts. In a smaller bowl, use a whisk to whip everything thoroughly until you achieve a smooth mixture.
2. Dip the cooled donuts into the frosting.
3. Before the frosting sets, sprinkle some chopped walnuts around the top of each.

Coco-Lime Cake Donuts

This recipe is an interesting way to make a tempting lime treat by adding lime on your homemade donut.

MAKES: 6 DONUTS
PREPARATION TIME: 15 minutes
BAKING TIME: 5 minutes

2 tablespoons cup milk
¼ tablespoon vinegar
½ cup all-purpose flour
6 tablespoons sugar
½ teaspoon baking powder
1 teaspoons lime zest
1/8 teaspoon salt
1 egg
2 tablespoons coconut milk
½ teaspoon vanilla extract
1 tablespoons unsalted butter

Topping:
juice of 1 lime
¼ cup powdered sugar
½ cup shredded coconut

Directions

1. Preheat oven to 350°F.
2. Lightly grease donut pan.
3. In a small bowl, combine vinegar and milk. Let it sit for about 5 minutes.
4. In a large bowl, mix together all dry ingredients.
5. In a medium bowl, lightly beat the remaining wet ingredients.
6. Combine butter and milk mixture.
7. Pour liquid combination to the dry mixture then stir until it forms a smooth batter.
8. Fill the prepared donut pan wells up to ¾ full with batter.
9. Bake for 5 to 8 minutes until donuts spring back when touched.
10. Let cool in pan for 5 minutes before transferring to wire rack.
11. Dip cooled donuts in glaze and sprinkle shredded coconut.

To make the topping

1. In a small bowl, whisk juice into powdered sugar to form glaze.
2. Make a thicker glaze to coat just the top of the donuts, or add a bit more of lime juice to make a thin glaze to cover sides as well.

Chunky Pineapple Mini Donuts

Chunks of the vitamin-packed pineapple will give color, texture and sweetness to these tiny donut snacks. Munch on all this goodness in one delicious bite.

MAKES: 12 MINI DONUTS
PREPARATION TIME: 5 minutes
BAKING TIME: 15 minutes

---

2 eggs, separated
¼ cup raw sugar aluminum-free
1 cup unbleached flour
1 teaspoon baking powder
½ cup chopped pineapple

Directions

1. Preheat the oven to 350°F.
2. Lightly grease a 12-hole mini donut pan.
3. Beat the yolks then whisk in the sugar.
4. Sift the flour over the yolks and then stir through.
5. Fold in the pineapple.
6. In a small bowl, beat the egg whites until stiff.
7. Fold the egg whites to the yolk and egg mixture then whisk until combined.
8. Equally divide the batter amongst the 12 donut pan holes. Make sure to include pineapple pieces in each pan well.

9. Bake for 15 minutes.
10. Allow to cool in the pan for a while before removing the donuts from the pan to cool completely.

Peachy White Chocolate Donuts

*This peachy white chocolate donut has a distinct and sweet fruity taste.
It will have your friends and family asking for more!*

MAKES: 6 DONUTS
PREPARATION TIME: 25 minutes
BAKING TIME: 12 minutes

---

1 tablespoon melted unsalted butter
1/3 cup plus 1 tablespoon buttermilk
1 egg, lightly beaten
1 cup cake flour, sifted
1/3 cup plus another 1 tablespoon of granulated sugar
1 teaspoon baking powder
pinch of nutmeg
½ teaspoon salt
½ cup peeled and diced peaches

For the glaze:
¼ cup white chocolate chips
1 teaspoon light corn syrup
1 tablespoon unsalted butter, diced
1 teaspoon water

Topping:
¼ cup unsweetened coconut flakes

Directions

1. Preheat oven to 350°F.
2. Place coconut flakes on a baking sheet and bake for 8 to12 minutes, stirring on half way, until coconut is toasted.
3. Increase oven heat to 400°F.
4. In a large bowl, whisk together the butter, beaten egg, and buttermilk.
5. In a separate medium bowl, whisk together all dry ingredients.
6. Incorporate the wet and dry ingredients mixture and stir to combine.
7. Fold in diced peaches.
8. Spoon batter into 6-count lightly greased donut pan. Fill each well to about two-thirds of the way full.
9. Bake for 8-12 minutes or until the tops of the donuts spring back when lightly pressed.
10. Allow to cool in the pan for a minute or two, then turn out donuts onto a cooling rack with wax paper below and let cool completely.

To make the glaze

1. Microwave all ingredients in a shallow bowl with 10 seconds interval time, stirring in between, until melted.
2. Dip cooled donuts into the slightly warm glaze and return to cooling rack for glaze to dry.
3. Top with toasted coconut.

Baked Peachy Cake Donut

Peach in the dough and peach in the glaze makes these donuts very fruity and sweet. The heavy cream makes the glaze very thick and mellow.

MAKES: 6 DONUTS
PREPARATION TIME: 10 minutes
BAKING TIME: 9 minutes

¾ cup flour
¼ cup sugar
1 teaspoon baking powder
¼ teaspoon cinnamon
¼ teaspoon salt
¼ cup milk
1 egg
1 tablespoon melted butter
¾ cup fresh peach, pureed
¾ tablespoon maple syrup

For the Glaze:
1¼ cups powdered sugar
1/3 cup heavy cream
1/3 cup of the peach puree
1 heaping tablespoon peach preserves

Directions

1. Preheat your oven to 425°F.
2. Grease a 6-count donut pan with nonstick cooking spray.
3. Combine the dry ingredients in a large bowl.
4. Form a well in the middle of the dry ingredients then add the milk, egg, maple syrup, and melted butter. Mix it until well-combined.
5. Add approximately ¼ cup of the pureed peaches. Batter should be wet, but not runny. You may add a bit more of the peach puree if necessary.
6. Pipe the batter into the donut pan, filling each well 2/3 of the way full.
7. Bake for 7-9 minutes or until the donuts are cooked through and edges turned golden brown.
8. Allow the donuts to cool in the pan for 2 or 3 minutes before removing to a cooling rack.

For the Peach Glaze

1. Combine all the ingredients in a bowl. You may add more puree or milk to thin the glaze to your desired consistency.
2. Once donuts are cooled completely, coat one side of each with the glaze.
3. When glazing the donuts, coat one side of it with the glaze and place back on the cooling racks while the glaze sets. Make sure to let the glaze set well.

Fruity Tropical Cake Donuts

*For an interesting taste, the delicious and tasty mango and kiwi are
sealed in the dough. Then a mixture of toasted coconut is used to make
a crispy and sweet topping.*

MAKES: 12 DONUTS
PREPARATION TIME: 10 minutes
BAKING TIME: 18 minutes

1 cup all-purpose flour
½ cup sugar
½ teaspoon salt
1 teaspoon baking powder
½ cup almond milk
1 tablespoon melted butter
½ teaspoon coconut extract
½ cup fresh kiwi, diced into small bits
½ cup fresh mango, diced into small bits

For the Glaze:
¾ cup powdered sugar
1 teaspoon coconut extract
1 tablespoon coconut milk
½ cup sweetened coconut

Directions

1. Preheat oven 350°F.

2. Lightly grease a donut pan.
3. In a large bowl, using an electric mixer or a whisk, mix the flour, sugar, salt and baking powder.
4. Add in the milk, butter and coconut extract. Mix it well to incorporate.
5. Stir in the mango and kiwi bits.
6. Place batter in a piping bag.
7. Fill each donut mold in the pan to about ¾ full.
8. Bake for 15-18 minutes or until donut springs back when touched and are slightly browned.
9. Remove pan from oven and let it cool for 5 minutes.
10. Use a thin spatula to remove the donuts from pan and place them on a wire rack to cool more.

For the glaze

1. In a small bowl mix the coconut extract and coconut milk. Whisk in the powdered sugar gradually until mixture is full blended and smooth.

For the toasted coconut

1. Take a cookie sheet and sprinkle a thin layer of sweetened coconut. Place on the middle rack of the oven toaster and watch it closely, it only takes less than 60 seconds for the coconut to toast.
2. Glaze each donuts and sprinkle with the toasted coconut.

Carrot Walnut Donuts

A lot is going on with this donut. Inside it, there is an awesome mixture of spices, pineapple, and carrot; then it is topped with a smooth and creamy frosting that is sprinkled with ground walnuts.

MAKES: 6 DONUTS
PREPARATION TIME: 15 minutes
BAKING TIME: 10 minutes

1½ tablespoons butter
3 tablespoons brown sugar
¼ teaspoon salt
1 egg
½ teaspoon vanilla extract
3 tablespoons vanilla yogurt
3 tablespoons crushed pineapple, drained (reserve the juice for frosting)
3 tablespoons finely shredded carrots
¾ cup all-purpose flour
¾ teaspoon ground cinnamon
¼ teaspoon nutmeg
½ teaspoon baking powder
½ teaspoon baking soda

Pineapple Cream Cheese Frosting:
¼ cup toasted walnuts, ground
3 tablespoons cream cheese, softened
1½ tablespoons butter, softened
1 tablespoon pineapple juice
¼ cup powdered sugar

Directions

1. Preheat oven to 375°F.
2. Spray donut pan with non-stick cooking spray.
3. Cream together butter, sugar and salt in large bowl.
4. Add egg, vanilla extract, and yogurt and beat until smooth.
5. Fold in pineapple and carrots.
6. Sift together all dry ingredients except for the walnuts.
7. Slowly add dry ingredients to wet ingredients, beating on low speed until well combined.
8. Fill a pastry bag with donut batter then snip off the tip.
9. Pipe batter into pan, filling wells to ½ full.
10. Bake for 10 minutes.
11. Let cool in pan before transferring to wire rack.
12. Frost cooled donuts as desired then sprinkle with ground walnuts.

To make the frosting

1. Place walnuts on a baking sheet and bake for about 8 minutes or until fragrant.
2. Let it cool on baking sheet.
3. Place baked walnuts in a food processor and pulse until walnuts are ground then set aside.
4. Beat cream cheese, butter and pineapple juice in medium bowl until smooth.
5. Slowly add powdered sugar until smooth.

Glazed Maraschino Cherry Donuts

This donut is loaded with sweet maraschino cherries and dunked in vanilla glaze. Sprinkles add fun on these nutmeg scented donuts. Enjoy the brilliant taste.

MAKES: 6 DONUTS
PREPARATION TIME: 10 minutes
BAKING TIME: 10 minutes

---

1 cup flour
6 tablespoons sugar
½ teaspoon baking powder
½ teaspoon baking soda
½ teaspoon kosher salt
¼ teaspoon ground nutmeg
1 egg
½ teaspoon vanilla extract
6 tablespoons skimmed milk
1 tablespoon butter, melted
8 maraschino cherries, chopped

For the Glaze:
1/8 cup heavy cream
½ teaspoon vanilla extract
1 1/8 cup powdered sugar
sprinkles

Directions

1. Preheat oven to 325°F.
2. Mix all dry ingredients except for the cherries. Add in all the wet ingredients one by one and whisk well until thoroughly combined. Fold in chopped cherries.
3. Pour batter into a sealable pastry bag and snip off one corner.
4. Pipe batter into greased donut pans.
5. Bake in for 10 minutes.
6. Remove from oven and allow it to cool in pans for 5 minutes before removing them to a cooling rack.

For the frosting

1. Heat the cream in a small saucepan until just before it begins to boil. Remove it from heat and whisk in vanilla extract and powdered sugar. Add more of cream or powdered sugar until desired consistency is reached.
2. Dip cooled donut into glaze.
3. Set on wax paper, apply sprinkles immediately.
4. Allow glaze to set for 15 minutes.

EVERYTHING 'IN-BETWEEN' DONUTS

Whole Wheat Lemon Greek Donuts

This Lemon Greek Donut recipe is super versatile and goes well with almost all sorts of beverages.

MAKES: 12 DONUTS
PREPARATION TIME: 15 minutes
BAKING TIME: 15 minutes

¼ cup butter
2 tablespoons of plain Greek yoghurt
1/3 cup milk
2 teaspoons of vanilla extract
1 egg
zest and juice of 1 lemon

½ cup sugar
¾ cup plain flour
½ cup whole wheat pastry flour
1½ teaspoon baking powder
¾ teaspoon baking soda
½ teaspoon of salt flakes

For the Glaze:
1 cup icing sugar
1 tablespoon of Greek yoghurt
1 tablespoon of milk
juice of ½ a lemon

Recommended Extra:
1 tablespoon of sugar
zest of ½ lemon

Directions

1. Preheat oven to 350°F.
2. In a medium bowl, whisk Greek yoghurt, milk, butter, egg, vanilla, lemon zest and juice until well combined.
3. Sift all dry ingredients into wet mixture and whisk until just combined.
4. Pour batter evenly into donut pan.
5. Bake for 12-15 minutes or until golden brown and the tops spring back when lightly pressed.
6. Allow to cool in tray for 10 minutes before transferring on a wire rack to cool completely.
7. Dunk each donut into the glaze then return on the rack. Finish with a sprinkle of lemon zest.

To make the glaze

1. In a small bowl combine sugar and lemon zest and stir to combine. Put this mixture aside.

2. In a separate bowl, sift icing sugar.
3. Squeeze in lemon juice, add Greek yoghurt, and milk on a teaspoon-at-a-time basis and stir until smooth.
4. Keep adding milk until you reach desired consistency.

Classic Cinnamon and Sugar Holes

Tempt your taste buds with this version of classic donut holes. It is dipped with butter then rolled in a perfect combination of cinnamon and sugar.

MAKES: 20 DONUT Holes
PREPARATION TIME: 10 minutes
BAKING TIME: 9 minutes

1/3 cup milk
1 teaspoon vinegar
½ cup unbleached all-purpose flour
3 tablespoons melted unsalted butter
½ cup white whole wheat flour
1 teaspoon baking powder, aluminum-free
¼ teaspoon sea salt
1/8 teaspoon nutmeg, fresh
¼ cup sugar
1 large egg
¼ vanilla bean
2 tablespoons honey

Topping:
5 tablespoons unsalted butter
1/3 cup pure cane sugar
1½ teaspoons cinnamon
1/3 c. powdered sugar

Directions

1. Preheat oven to 400°F.
2. In a small bowl, mix together vinegar and milk. Allow to sit for about 5 minutes.
3. Whisk together flours, baking powder, sea salt, and nutmeg using a large mixing bowl, and then set aside this mixture.
4. Mix butter, sugar, honey, vanilla bean seeds, and egg until evenly combined.
5. Add in curdled milk.
6. Whisk together wet and dry ingredients until just combined.
7. Grease a mini muffin tin pan then evenly distribute batter.
8. Bake for 9 minutes.
9. Allow to cool at least 1 minute before removing from tin and placing on a cooling rack to cool.

For the topping

1. In a small bowl, mix together cinnamon and sugar. Then in a separate bowl, add in powdered sugar.
2. Dip each donut hole in butter before coating 10 holes in cinnamon and sugar mixture, and the other 10 to the powdered sugar mixture.
3. Place back on cooling rack until dried.

Double Maple Donut

With maple syrup in the dough and maple syrup glaze, this donut is a maple treat inside and out. It's perfect for gluten-free dieters and maple lovers as well.

MAKES: 6 DONUTS
PREPARATION TIME: 25 minutes
BAKING TIME: 10 minutes

½ cup coconut flour
½ teaspoon baking soda
1/8 teaspoon   salt
1 whole egg
2 egg whites
2 tablespoons low sugar maple syrup
1 teaspoon maple extract
2 tablespoon   unsweetened applesauce
½ cup skim milk
½ cup sweetener of choice

Maple Glaze:
¼ cup ideal powdered sugar
¼ teaspoon maple extract
1 teaspoon water

Directions

1.   Preheat oven to 350°F.

2. Spray a donut pan with cooking spray.
3. In a medium size bowl, mix together the dry ingredients.
4. In a separate bowl, mix together the wet ingredients.
5. Combine the wet and dry ingredients, and mix until batter is smooth and lump-free.
6. Divide batter evenly between the 6 donut molds.
7. Bake for 20-25 minutes or until toothpick comes out clean.

For the glaze

1. Mix all 3 ingredients until smooth in a small bowl. Use a ½ teaspoon measure to spoon glaze over the top of each donut.

Buttered Cinnamon Donuts

It is said that some of the best things in life are simple. Try this Buttered Cinnamon donut and enjoy elegant simplicity!

MAKES: 6 DONUTS
PREPARATION TIME: 10 minutes
BAKING TIME: 17 minutes

Baking spray with flour
1 cup all-purpose flour
¾ cup sugar
1 teaspoon baking powder
½ teaspoon ground cinnamon
¼ teaspoon ground nutmeg
¼ teaspoon kosher salt
1 egg, lightly beaten
1 cup whole milk
1 tablespoon unsalted butter, melted
1 teaspoon pure vanilla extract

For the topping:
¼ cup unsalted butter
¼ cup sugar
¼ teaspoon ground cinnamon

Directions

1.   Preheat the oven to 350°F.

2. Spray 2 donut pans well.
3. In a large bowl, mix flour, baking powder, cinnamon, sugar, nutmeg, and salt all together.
4. In a smaller bowl, whisk together egg, milk, vanilla, and the melted butter.
5. Stir the wet mixture into the dry ingredients until well combined.
6. Spoon the batter into the baking pans; filling each one a little more than three-quarters full.
7. Bake for 17 minutes or until a toothpick comes out clean.
8. Allow to cool for 5 minutes, and then tap the donuts out onto a sheet pan.

For the topping
1. Melt the butter in a small sauté pan. Combine the sugar and cinnamon in a small mixing bowl.
2. Brush the top of each donut with butter and then coat in the cinnamon sugar.

Red Bean Surprise Donuts

With Adzuki red beans this recipe makes a surprisingly delicious donut dessert that you'll be happy to enjoy.

MAKES: 12 MINI DONUTS
PREPARATION TIME: 10 minutes
BAKING TIME: 10 minutes

¾ cup whole wheat pastry flour
¼ teaspoon baking soda
¼ teaspoon baking powder
¼ teaspoon salt
⅔ cup unsweetened nondairy milk
⅔ cup Sweet red bean paste
¼ teaspoon apple cider vinegar

For the Sweet Red Bean Paste:
1 cup dry adzuki beans
3 cups water
1 cup sugar

Directions

1. Preheat the oven to 350°F.
2. Grease a mini donut pan.

3. Sift together all dry ingredients then set it aside.
4. Add all the wet ingredients including the bean paste to a small bowl and whisk.
5. Pour the wet ingredients to the dry ingredients and mix using a wooden spoon.
6. Mix batter thoroughly but never over mix it.
7. Use a small cookie scoop to spoon the batter into a mini-donut pan.
8. Bake for 10 minutes.
9. Let donuts cool in the pan for few minutes before removing them.

To make the bean paste

1. Put beans and water in a saucepan and bring to a boil.
2. Decrease the heat to low, cover, and cook until the beans are soft for about an hour or two.
3. Once the beans are cooked, add the sugar and stir to combine.
4. Keep cooking until the beans are thick.
5. Blend the paste in a food processor till smooth.
6. Leftovers can be stored in the fridge for a week.

Coco-Nut Donuts

This recipe whips up in no time, no advanced baking skills required. Plus the coconut flavored frosting is really easy, and as we all know everything gets better with frosting.

MAKES: 6 DONUTS
PREPARATION TIME: 10 minutes
BAKING TIME: 20 minutes

2 tablespoons water
¼ cup maple syrup
2 tablespoons coconut oil
¼ cup full fat coconut milk
2 tablespoons ground flaxseed
1 cup whole wheat pastry flour
2 teaspoons gluten-free baking powder

Date Frosting and Toasted Coconut Topping:
¼ cup coconut, shredded and unsweetened
¼ cup or 8 pieces dried dates
¼ cup coconut oil

Directions

1. Preheat the oven to 350 °F.
2. Combine and mix all dry ingredients in a medium

bowl. Combine and mix also all wet ingredients in small bowl.

3. Add the wet to the dry mixture and mix everything well, but do not overdo as the donuts may get tough if you overdo the mixing.
4. Spray oil to the donut pan.
5. Spoon the batter evenly into the pan holes.
6. Bake for about 20 minutes or until a toothpick comes out clean.
7. Allow to cool slightly.

For the frosting

1. Blend dates and oil together in a food processor.
2. Spread or dip the donuts into the frosting and top with the coconut.

Cookies 'N' Cream Donuts

This cookies 'n' cream donut makes the perfect snack or dessert with a glass of milk. I like to call these 'my oreo donuts'.

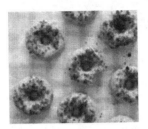

MAKES: 6 DONUTS
PREPARATION TIME: 10 minutes
BAKING TIME: 12 minutes

¾ cups cake flour
1/3 cup sugar
1 teaspoons baking powder
1/3 teaspoon salt
1/3 cup cream
1 egg
1/3 tablespoon vanilla
2 tablespoons melted butter
3 tablespoons cookies and cream pieces

For the Glaze and Topping:

1/3 cup powdered sugar
2 tablespoons cream
½ teaspoon vanilla
3 tablespoons chocolate and cream sandwich cookies, that is coarsely crushed

Directions

1. Preheat the oven to 350°F.
2. Grease a donut pan well with baking spray.
3. Chop the cookies and cream pieces and then set aside.
4. Sift together all of the dry ingredients in a large bowl.
5. In a smaller bowl, whisk together the cream, eggs, vanilla and butter.
6. Pour the wet ingredients into the dry ingredients mixture and fold the batter until well combined.
7. Fold in the cookies and cream pieces.
8. Spoon the batter into the greased pan.
9. Bake for 10-12 minutes or until just cooked through and the tops are golden.
10. Let the donuts cool completely on a wire rack after allowing them to cool for a while in the pan.
11. While the donuts are cooling, go and prepare the glaze.
12. Dip the cooled donuts in the glaze until they have a nice thick coating.
13. Generously sprinkle on the crushed cookie sandwich chunks and crumbs.

To make the glaze
1. Whisk the cream, vanilla and powdered sugar together.

Lemon Poppy Seeds Donuts

These cute and tiny poppy seeds add fun with to these lemony flavored donuts. These are a sure win for everybody's palate

MAKES: 6 DONUTS
PREPARATION TIME: 10 minutes
BAKING TIME: 18 minutes

---

1 cup unbleached all-purpose flour
1 teaspoon baking powder
½ cup sugar
¼ teaspoon salt
1 tablespoon poppy seeds
½ cup buttermilk
2 tablespoons butter
1 teaspoon vanilla extract
1 large egg
zest from 1 lemon

For the glaze:
1/8 cup lemon juice
1 cup powdered sugar

Directions

2. Preheat the oven to 350°F.

3. In a medium bowl, combine the flour, baking powder, salt, poppy seeds, and the sugar.
4. In a 2-cup measuring bowl, whisk together the egg, buttermilk, butter, vanilla extract, and lemon zest too.
5. Pour the wet ingredients into the dry ingredients and mix with a wooden spatula until well combined.
6. Grease your 6-count donut pan with cooking oil or spray.
7. Fill each mold about halfway full with batter.
8. Bake for 15 to 18 minutes, or until a toothpick inserted into the donut comes out clean.
9. Remove the pan from the oven and let it cool completely.

For the glaze

1. Whisk the lemon juice and powdered sugar until they form a thin paste.
2. Place a cookie sheet under baking rack. When the donuts have completely cooled, flip the pan onto the rack to release donuts.
3. One by one, dip the donuts into the glaze and let them dry on the rack.

Caramel Frost and Toffee Sunday

This is such a mouth-watering donut with a rich caramel frosting. It is then topped with a drizzle of chocolate and a sprinkle of toffee pieces.

MAKES: 6 DONUTS
PREPARATION TIME: 10 minutes
BAKING TIME: 9 minutes

1 cup flour
½ cup sugar
¼ cup cocoa powder
¼ cup mini chocolate chips (optional)
½ teaspoon baking soda
½teaspoon vanilla extract
1 egg
6 tablespoons sour cream
¼ cup milk
¼ cup vegetable oil

Frosting:
¼ cup unsalted butter
1 cup powdered sugar
1 tablespoon heavy cream or milk
1 tablespoon caramel sauce
pinch kosher salt

Chocolate Sundae Topping:
¼ cup semi-sweet chocolate chips
2 tablespoons unsalted butter
1 tablespoon vegetable oil
¼ cup toffee pieces

Directions

1. Preheat oven to 400°F.
2. In a small bowl mix all dry ingredients well. Allow it to sit for about 5 minutes.
3. Whisk together all wet ingredients in a large mixing bowl.
4. Add the wet ingredients to the dry mixture and combine well.
5. Grease a donut pan then evenly distribute the batter.
6. Bake for 8 minutes or test with a toothpick if it's done. Toothpick should come out clean when inserted.
7. Allow to cool at least 1 minute before removing from tin and placing on a cooling rack to cool.
8. Cream the butter, powdered sugar, caramel sauce, cream, and salt together until it's light and fluffy.
9. Frost tops of the cooled donuts.

For the Topping

1. In a small sauce pan, melt together the chocolate chips, oil, and butter over low heat. Stir it constantly and remove it from heat as soon as everything is melted and combined.
2. Use a spoon to drizzle the chocolate topping over the each donut.
3. Sprinkle the toffee pieces over the top.

Pumpkin Spiced Donut Holes

*These irresistible and tasty pumpkin spiced donut holes are flavorful.
These soft and tasty donuts are rolled in a mixture of pumpkin pie spice
and sugar.*

MAKES: 20 DONUT Holes
PREPARATION TIME: 10 minutes
BAKING TIME: 15 minutes

*2 cups all-purpose flour
1 cup sugar
1 teaspoon baking soda
1 teaspoon baking powder
pinch of salt
2 eggs
½ cup heavy cream
¼ cup whole milk
2 tablespoons coconut oil, melted and slightly cooled
1 teaspoon vanilla bean paste
4 tablespoons melted butter
½ cup sugar
3 teaspoons pumpkin pie spice*

Directions

1. Preheat oven to 350°F.
2. Lightly oil the donut pan with a little baking spray or coconut oil.

3. Mix the flour, sugar, salt, baking powder, and the baking soda in a large bowl.
4. In a small bowl, beat the eggs, milk coconut oil, cream, and vanilla bean paste together using a fork.
5. Add it to the dry ingredients.
6. Mix everything together until moist.
7. Scoop the dough into a large pastry bag. Trim off a small corner of the end of the bag.
8. Pipe some dough into each cavity of the donut pan.
9. Only fill up each little hole about half way.
10. Bake 10–15 minutes until golden browned.
11. Remove from the oven and let cool for 3 minutes, then remove the holes from the pan.
12. Combine the sugar and pumpkin pie spice together in a small mixing bowl.
13. Using a pastry brush, brush butter on each donut hole, then roll them in the sugar mixture one by one.

Caramel Twist Donut Cakes

The donut topping goes well with the caramel glaze. It neutralizes the heavy sweetness of the chocolate donut and adds to the unique taste.

MAKES: 6 DONUTS
PREPARATION TIME: 15 minutes
BAKING TIME: 12 minutes

½ cup all-purpose flour
2 tablespoons cocoa powder
4 tablespoons butter
½ teaspoon baking powder
1 large egg
5 tablespoons canola oil
1 tablespoon packed dark-brown sugar
½ teaspoon vanilla extract
4 tablespoons granulated sugar

For the Brown Butter Caramel Glaze:
4 tablespoons butter
4 tablespoons packed brown sugar
5 tablespoons half & half
½ cup powdered sugar
½ teaspoon vanilla extract
Flaky sea salt, for garnish

Directions

1. Preheat oven to 325° F.
2. Brush donut pan with some melted butter.
3. In a heavy-bottomed pan, melt butter over medium heat until it looks golden brown. Remove from heat instantly and set aside.
4. Whisk together flour, and baking powder, and cocoa powder in a small bowl. Set it aside.
5. In the bowl of an electric mixer fitted with a whisk attachment, whip the egg with the sugars until light and thickened for about 5 minutes. Stir in the dry ingredients until perfectly blended. Add browned butter, vanilla, and oil; stir to incorporate. Then set aside to rest for 10 minutes.
6. Put batter to a pastry bag. Trim a ½-inch hole in one tip. Pipe batter evenly into the 6-cavity donut pan. Bake at the oven's middle rack for 10 minutes. Let pan cool on a wire rack for 10 minutes before gently removing the donuts from it.

For the glaze

1. Melt butter over medium heat until golden brown in a heavy-bottomed sauce pan. Instantly add half & half and brown sugar. Whisk to combine, and then bring to a boil. Let it boil for a minute. Remove from heat and add vanilla extract and powdered sugar. Whisk continuously for 1 minute until glaze is smooth. Instantly transfer to a small bowl with a mouth wider than the donuts.
2. Dip the bottom side of the donuts in the glaze. Turn it right-side up and place on a wire rack to set. Sprinkle donuts with a bit of flaky sea salt while glaze is still wet.

Signature Vanilla Almond Donuts

Preparation Time: 15 Minutes
Baking Time: 7 Minutes
Makes: 6 Donuts

1/3 cup Almond Milk
1 teaspoon White Vinegar
3 tablespoons Unsalted Butter
½ cup White Whole Wheat Flour (unbleached)
½ cup Unbleached All-purpose Flour
1 teaspoon Baking Powder (use aluminum free brand)
¼ teaspoon Salt
1/8 teaspoon Freshly Grated Nutmeg
¼ cup Light Brown Sugar
2 tablespoons Honey
1 large Egg
1 teaspoon Vanilla Extract

Glaze Topping Ingredients:
1 tablespoon half and half or half Cream (blend of equal parts of half
heavy cream and half whole milk)
1 teaspoon Vanilla Extract
¼ cup + 2 tablespoons Powdered Sugar
¼ cup crushed Almonds

Directions

1. Preheat your to 400 degrees Fahrenheit. Prepare a nonstick 6-cavity donut pan with cooking spray.
2. Mix the almond milk and white vinegar in a bowl. Let it sit for about 5 minutes until it curdles.
3. In a small saucepan on low flame, melt the butter, pour it in a bowl and place it aside for cooling.

4. In the meanwhile, get a large bowl and add the following: unbleached white whole wheat flour, unbleached all-purpose flour, baking powder, sea salt. Whisk together sell and place aside.
5. Add in the sugar, honey, vanilla extract, eggs to the cooled melted butter and whisk together until ingredients are evenly combined. Pour in the curdled milk mixture.
6. Gently whisk to combine the wet mixture with the dry ingredients without overdoing it. Quick Note: Excessive mixing could result in a hard-dense donut.
7. Use a piping bag to evenly pipe the donut batter in each cavity in the pan about half full.
8. Allow donuts to bake for 7 minutes. Remove donut pan from the oven and allow cooling for about a minute before removing donuts and placing them on a cooling rack for about 15 minutes.

Preparing the glaze

1. Note: the glaze should be prepared while the donuts are cooling.
2. In a bowl, add the half and half cream and vanilla extract and whisk together well ensuring that it is evenly mixed.
3. Gradually add in the powdered sugar and mix until a smooth texture is achieved. If your glaze turns out with too much thickness, an extra teaspoon or more of half and half cream can fix it. If the glaze has a consistency that is too thin, an extra tablespoon or more of powdered sugar can fix it. Note: any extra cream or sugar must be added one at a time and combined to check for consistency before adding more.
4. As soon as donuts have been totally cooled, dunk or dip each donut in the glaze while swirling around the donut in the bowl in order to evenly coat it.
5. After it is evenly coated with the glaze, evenly sprinkle with crushed almonds.

6. Return glazed and almond coated donuts to cooling rack and let it sit and dry for approximately 20 minutes drying time.
7. Serve the same day and lightly cover any leftovers to store it.

Ginger Sweet Donuts

Spice up your day with this sweet and minty donut that's got ginger in the dough and ginger on top. It is the new ring ginger bread you'll love.

MAKES: 12 DONUTS
PREPARATION TIME: 10 minutes
BAKING TIME: 22 minutes

½ cup sweet rice flour
1/3 cup pure cane sugar
3 tablespoons almond meal
½ cup oat flour
2 teaspoons ginger
1½ teaspoons cinnamon
½ teaspoon ground cloves
½ teaspoon salt
¼ teaspoon black pepper
2 large eggs
1 teaspoon baking powder
½ teaspoon nutmeg
1/3 cup milk
3 tablespoons unsweetened applesauce
2 tablespoons molasses
2 tablespoons oil
1½ teaspoons vanilla extract

Glaze:
1 cup powdered sugar
2-3 tablespoons milk
¼ teaspoon cinnamon
¼ teaspoon ginger

1/8 teaspoon ground cloves

Directions

1. Preheat your oven to 350° F.
2. Grease a donut pan.
3. Combine the sweet rice flour, cane sugar, almond meal, oat flour, ginger, cinnamon, baking powder, nutmeg, ground cloves, black pepper, and salt in a large bowl, mixing all of it well.
4. Whisk the eggs together in a separate bowl. Then add in the milk, molasses, oil, vanilla extract, and applesauce. Whisk well until all is combined.
5. Pour the wet mixture into the dry and stir using a large wooden spoon until just combined, but be careful not to over mix it.
6. Spoon the batter into the donut molds, filing to just below the top of every mold.
7. Bake for 18-22 minutes until edges are lightly golden brown. Testing it with a toothpick inserted in the center should come out clean. Let cool in the pan for 5 minutes. Use a thin spatula to help loosen them out, and place on a cooling rack to cool fully before glazing.

For the glaze

1. Mix ingredients together in a bowl until smooth. You may add more milk if a thinner consistency is desired. Dip the donut into the glaze and let the excess drip off. Set until glaze is hardened.

Cinna-Mini Rings

Take a bite of these wheat-free mini donuts. This delectable and also unusual taste is sure to please.

MAKES: 12 DONUTS
PREPARATION TIME: 15 minutes
BAKING TIME: 13 -15 minutes

1/3 cup coconut flour
1/3 cup potato starch
1 teaspoon baking soda
1 teaspoon gluten-free baking powder
1/3 cup sugar
1/3 teaspoon vanilla bean powder
2 tablespoons, 2 teaspoons coconut oil
2 teaspoons vanilla bean extract
½ cup coconut milk

Topping:
1 tablespoon, 1 teaspoon coconut oil
2/3 cup sugar
1 tablespoon, 1 teaspoon cinnamon

Directions

1. In a medium-sized bowl pour all of the dry ingredients and whisk together. Then stir in the

coconut oil, milk and vanilla extract. Mix everything together, continuing until the batter turns smooth. The batter must be slightly thick with a smooth light texture.

2. Start scooping about 1½ tablespoons of batter into each mini-donut pan. You may use a cookie scoop to help with the scooping.

3. Bake in a 325°F-preheated oven for around 10-13 minutes. Then test and see if they feel done. Carefully remove them from the pan with a knife and place on a plate.

For the Topping

1. Mix cinnamon and sugar in a bowl. Lightly coat each donut in about 1 tablespoon of coconut oil and toss them in the cinnamon sugar mixture.

Vanilla Cake Donut Holes

Maybe going through the long process of setting the dough for these donuts may sound tiring, but it's all worth the waiting. You will enjoy one of the most delightful tasting treat after it all.

MAKES: 12 DONUTS
PREPARATION TIME: 2 hrs. and 40 min.
BAKING TIME: 12 minutes
NOTE: set dough overnight

2 cups soymilk
¼ cup vegetable oil
¼ cup maple syrup
½ cup sugar
2½ teaspoons yeast
1 teaspoon vanilla
¼ cup applesauce
1 teaspoon salt
4½ cups flour – a combination of 3 cups white unbleached flour and 1½ cup of whole wheat flour

Vanilla Glaze:
1 cup powdered sugar
2 tablespoons soy milk
½ teaspoon vanilla essence

Chocolate Glaze:
1 cup powdered sugar
⅓ cup cocoa

3 tablespoons soy milk

Directions

1. Combine soy milk, vegetable oil, sugar, and maple syrup in a small sauce pan and bring to a boil. Let cool till 110°F or test it with your clean finger, it must be as warm as your finger. This cooling process may take an hour or more.
2. Once the soy milk mixture has reached the required temperature, stir in the yeast and let it sit for 10 minutes.
3. In a large bowl, stir the 4 cups of flour and the 1 teaspoon of salt. Add the soy milk/yeast mix to the flour. Mix well and let the dough rise for an hour until it's about double in size.
4. After the dough has risen, add the remaining ½ cup of flour, vanilla, and applesauce. Mix well and then let the dough sit for another 10 minutes. This dough is very sticky, but this will give you the best results you want to work with.
5. Flour a working surface and your hands and start creating dough balls – about 2-inch sizes. Place balls on greased cookie sheets and be sure to allow room for expansion.
6. Place a light-weight kitchen towel over your cookie sheets and place in the fridge overnight.
7. The next morning, turn your oven on to its lowest setting.
8. Then place the cookie sheets in the oven and then turn the off the heat and close the door. Allow the donuts to rest, anywhere from 30 minutes to an hour.
9. Heat the oven to 350°F.
10. Bake for about 10-12 minutes or until the tops are golden brown.

For the glaze

1. Mix together all ingredients for each glaze until smooth.
2. Once the donuts are out of the oven, let them cool enough so that you can handle them.
3. Dip each directly into the glaze. Icing the donuts while they're still warm helps the glaze settle well.
4. You may add sprinkles or nuts or any topping you like.
5. Cover and let it set for 15 minutes.

Honey Vanilla Donuts

These light honey donuts are glazed with heaven-scented vanilla beans.
These can be truly a stress buster with a cup of tea or coffee!

MAKES: 6 DONUTS
PREPARATION TIME: 5 minutes
BAKING TIME: 7 minutes

1/3 cup milk
1 teaspoon vinegar
3 tablespoons unsalted butter
½ cup white whole wheat flour
½ cup unbleached all-purpose flour
1 teaspoon baking powder that is aluminum-free
¼ teaspoon sea salt
1/8 teaspoon nutmeg, fresh
¼ cup sugar
2 tablespoons honey
1 large egg
¼ vanilla bean

Glaze:
1 tablespoons half and half
¼ vanilla bean
½ cup powdered sugar

Directions

1. Preheat oven to 400°F.
2. In a small bowl, mix together milk and vinegar. Allow it to sit for about 5 minutes to curdle.
3. Meanwhile, whisk together baking powder, flours, sea salt, and nutmeg in a large bowl.
4. In a separate bowl, whisk in sugar, honey, egg, melted butter, and vanilla bean seeds until thoroughly combined. Add in the curdled milk.
5. Whisk together wet and dry ingredients mixtures until just combined.
6. Spray donut pan.
7. Add batter to a piping bag and pipe evenly into each well in the pan.
8. Bake for 7 minutes.
9. Allow to cool 1 minute in the pan before turning it over to remove donuts onto a cooling rack.

For the glaze

1. In a flat-bottomed bowl, whisk together vanilla bean seeds and half and half until thoroughly combined. Slowly mix in powdered sugar and whisk until smooth. If glaze is too thick you may add 1 teaspoon more of half and half at a time. And if dough is too thin, add 1 tablespoon more of powdered sugar at a time.
2. Once donuts have completely cooled, about 15-20 minutes, dunk each in the glaze rocking the donut around the bowl to evenly coat.
3. Place back on cooling rack and allow drying for about 20 minutes.

Vanilla Spiced Donut

A cup of black coffee would be a perfect match for these sweet donuts.
These make a great choice for mid-day snack.

MAKES: 12 DONUTS
PREPARATION TIME: 10 minutes
BAKING TIME: 10 minutes

¼ cup butter
¼ cup vegetable oil
½ cup granulated sugar
1/3 cup brown sugar
2 large eggs
1 teaspoon vanilla extract
½ teaspoon ground nutmeg
2 2/3 cups all-purpose gluten-free baking mix
1 cup milk

Topping:
½ cup confectioners' sugar

Directions

1. Preheat the oven to 425°F.
2. Lightly grease two regular donut pans.
3. Use a medium-sized bowl and beat together the butter, vegetable oil, and sugars until its smooth. Add in the eggs, beating to combine. Stir in nutmeg,

vanilla, gluten-free baking mix and milk into the batter. Alternately pour baking mix and milk, starting and ending with the baking mix. Make sure everything is thoroughly combined but avoid over mixing.

4. Place the batter to the greased donut pans, filling the cavities up to ¼-inch below the rim. A teaspoon cookie scoop helps well for this.

5. Bake the donuts for 10 minutes or until set. Remove them from the oven, and wait for 7 minutes before placing them onto a rack. Let cool completely.

6. Shake donuts in a paper or plastic bag with about ½ cup confectioners' sugar.

Butterscotch Frosted Cake Donuts

A classic donut treated with an elegant butterscotch glaze. You can pick your choice of toppings and give yourself a pampering donut treat.

MAKES: 6 DONUTS
PREPARATION TIME: 10 minutes
BAKING TIME: 10 minutes

2/3 cup all-purpose gluten free flour
1/3 cup cocoa powder
1/3 cup granulated sugar
1 teaspoon baking powder
½ teaspoon baking soda
¼ teaspoon salt
¼ teaspoon ground nutmeg
¼ teaspoon xanthan gum
¼ cup canola oil
¼ cup unsweetened applesauce
1 egg
¼ cup milk substitute or milk
2 teaspoons vanilla extract

Butterscotch Glaze:
¾ cup packed dark brown sugar
¼ teaspoon salt
¼ cup vegan margarine
¼ cup coconut milk, unsweetened
2 teaspoons vanilla extract
3 tablespoons powdered sugar, sifted

Other optional topping ideas if you have a nut allergy:
toasted coconut
crisp rice cereal
sea salt
sprinkles

Directions

1. Preheat oven to 350 degrees.
2. Grease a 6-count, non-stick donut pan with pan spray.
3. In the bowl of a standing mixer fitted with the paddle attachment combine the dry ingredients on slow speed to evenly distribute.
4. Add in canola oil, applesauce, milk, egg, and vanilla. Mix on medium-low for about 1 minute or until thoroughly combined; it should have the consistency of a cake batter.
5. Scrape batter into a piping bag and pipe batter into prepared donut pan.
6. Bake in center of oven for 10 minutes or until donuts spring back a bit when lightly touched.
7. Cool for a minute or two in the pan on a wire rack before carefully turning the donuts into wire rack.

For the glaze

1. In a medium-sized saucepan melt brown sugar, margarine, and coconut milk slowly over medium-low heat. Stir it constantly with a whisk. After the mixture is melted, increase the heat and allow it to come to a boil for 6-8 minutes, continuing to whisk constantly. Remove it from heat and whisk in vanilla and the powdered sugar. Let the glaze cool in the refrigerator until the mixture has thickened, still stirring occasionally.
2. When the glaze is at desired thickness, dip the cooled

donuts and top with almonds. Allow glaze to set a bit.

Whole Wheat Chocolate Donuts

Treat your family with these nutritious chocolaty baked whole wheat donuts. You will surely be glad they are enjoying a healthier version of this classic favorite.

MAKES: 6 DONUTS
PREPARATION TIME: 10 minutes
BAKING TIME: 22 minutes

½ cup whole wheat pastry flour
¼ cup oat flour
1/8 cup barley flour
1/8 cup cocoa powder
½ cup unrefined sugar
1 egg
½ teaspoon aluminum free baking powder
¼ teaspoon aluminum free baking soda
½ cup low-fat milk
1 tablespoon olive oil
3 tablespoons dark chocolate chips
½ teaspoon chocolate extract

To decorate:
4 tablespoons white chocolate chips

Directions

1. Preheat oven to 325°F.
2. Prepare pan by spraying it with cooking oil or butter.

3. In a bowl, whisk eggs, milk, sugar, the chocolate extract, and oil.
4. Add flours, baking powder, baking soda, and cocoa powder. Whisk it until combined.
5. Carefully fold in the chocolate chips.
6. Put the batter in a piping bag and fill each donut hole to 2/3 full.
7. Bake for 17-22 minutes.
8. Cool for about 10 minutes in the pan and remove them to a wire rack.
9. Allow to cool completely.

For the glaze

1. Melt the chocolate chips in the microwave 30 seconds at a time making sure to mix in between each 30 seconds. It may take 1 minute and 30 seconds.
2. Use a method of your choice to make a decorative effect on the donuts.

Jam-filled Baked Donuts

Pick your choice of jam to fill these fabulous baked mini donuts. You can have it in a meal as a snack.

MAKES: 12 DONUTS Holes
PREPARATION TIME: 10 minutes
BAKING TIME: 10 minutes

200 grams strong white bread flour
1 heaped tablespoon caster sugar
pinch of salt
25 grams butter
1 teaspoon fast action yeast
1 egg
5 tablespoons milk
4 tablespoons jam of your choice

For the coating:
3 tablespoons icing sugar
2 tablespoons cold water
6 tablespoons caster sugar

Directions

1.   Preheat oven to 180°C.

2. In a large bowl, mix together the flour, sugar and salt then pour in the melted butter.
3. Heat the milk for 20 seconds in the microwave.
4. Add yeast, beaten egg and heated milk to the flour mixture and mix well until it forms to soft dough.
5. Turn out onto a floured surface and knead for 5 minutes.
6. Place back in bowl, cover bowl with cling wrap and allow it to rise for 1 hour.
7. Knock the dough back then split it into 12 equal sized balls.
8. Flatten out each ball until it is a disk with approximately 9cm in diameter.
9. Place a teaspoon of jam in the center then fold over the edges of the dough to encase the jam. Use a small amount of water to help seal the dough.
10. Place them, well-spaced, on a lined baking tray.
11. Cover and allow it to rise again for 30 minutes.
12. Bake for 10 minutes or until the donuts are risen and golden in color.
13. Allow to cool for 10 minutes while you make the topping.

For the topping
1. Mix together icing sugar and water in a bowl.
2. Dip the cooled donuts in this sugary mixture first then coat in the caster sugar.
3. Allow to dry and cool.

Baked Lemonade Donuts

If you haven't had a chance to go to the grocery store, but you want to bake a snack? If you have some lemonade powder plus a few other ingredients, this could be the right one for you. All ingredients for this are probably already available in your cupboard.

MAKES: 6 DONUTS
PREPARATION TIME: 7 minutes
BAKING TIME: 10 minutes

---

1 cup all-purpose flour
¼ cup granulated sugar
1 teaspoon baking powder
½ teaspoon salt
1 package (13 ounces) pink lemonade powder
¼ cup milk
1 egg
½ teaspoon vanilla extract
½ teaspoon unsalted butter

Lemonade Glaze:
1¼ cups powdered sugar
1/8 teaspoon lemonade powder
2 tablespoons milk
yellow food gel

Directions

1. Preheat oven to 325°F.
2. Grease a heart-shaped or a regular donut pan.
3. In a large mixing bowl, whisk together all dry ingredients.
4. Stir in the wet ingredients then mix until completely combined.
5. Fill donut cavities 2/3 of the way full.
6. Bake for 8-10 minutes, or until the tops of the donuts spring back when lightly pressed.
7. Let donuts cool for a while in the pan after removing from the oven.
8. Transfer to a wire rack to cool completely before glazing them.

For the glaze

1. Combine powdered sugar and lemonade powder. Add milk until you've reached a desired drizzling consistency. Stir in a drop of yellow food gel.
2. Using a fork or spoon, drizzle glaze over each of the cooled donuts.

Caramel-Cinnamon Sweet Potato Donuts

Have you tried a sweet potato pie? Well, if you have tried it and liked it, this sweet potato treat is for you. Enjoy this sweet potato cinnamon goodness.

MAKES: 6 DONUTS
PREPARATION TIME: 2 hours
BAKING TIME: 20 minutes

1 cup boiled sweet potato, mashed
3¼ cup all-purpose flour
2 teaspoon yeast
½ teaspoon salt
2 tablespoon sugar
2 tablespoon butter
1 teaspoon ground cinnamon
¾ cup warm water
¼ cup unsweetened coconut flakes

Caramel-Cinnamon Glaze:
4 tablespoons unsalted butter
½ cup granulated sugar
¼ cup milk
½ teaspoon salt
½ teaspoon ground cinnamon
½ to ¾ cup confectioner's sugar

Directions

1. In a large mixing bowl mix with paddle attachment, mix all ingredients except the flour until they're combined.
2. Switch to the hook attachment and add the flour 1 cup at a time until you get a nice and smooth dough.
3. Cover the bowl with a dry kitchen towel and let it rise for an hour or so at a warm place until size doubles.
4. Push down the dough and remove onto a floured work tabletop. Roll out the dough to approximately 1/4-inch thick.
5. Cut the dough out with a donut cutter. Gather the donut holes and dough scraps and re-roll them to cut and get out more donuts.
6. Place donuts on parchment paper, cover with cling wrap and place in warp spot and let rise for 20 minutes or until they seem light and spongy.
7. While waiting, preheat the oven to 400°F.

Prepare the glaze

1. In a small saucepan over medium heat, stir butter, granulated sugar, and salt all together. At the time the sugar is caramelized, whisk in the milk until you get a smooth caramel sauce. Set it aside to cool for 10 to 15 minutes. Add in the cinnamon and stir. Add in the sugar, 2 tablespoon at a time until you reach a thick consistency. Mix well to remove all lumps. Set at one aside.
2. Bake the donuts in the center of the oven for about 15 to 20 minutes.
3. When it's done, let it cool for a while.
4. Dip tops of donuts into the glaze.
5. Place on a wire rack or cookie sheet to allow glaze to set.

SPECIAL OCCASION / HOLIDAY DONUTS

Frosty Red Velvet Valentine Donuts

The cream cheese on these baked donuts makes it a very thick and rich frosting-like glaze. These Valentine's treat are sure to make anyone fall in love again.

MAKES: 6 DONUTS
PREPARATION TIME: 5 minutes
BAKING TIME: 10 minutes

---

1 1/3 cup red velvet dry cake mix
1/3 cup buttermilk
1 tablespoon oil
1 egg, beaten

For the frosting:
4 ounces cream cheese, at room temperature
½ cup powdered sugar
1 tablespoon heavy cream

187

¼ teaspoon vanilla

Garnish:
Valentine Sprinkles

Directions

1. Preheat the oven to 350°F.
2. Spray a donut pan with non-stick spray.
3. In a large bowl, whisk together all of the dry ingredients.
4. In smaller bowl, sift all dry ingredients then mix well to combine.
5. Create a well in the center of the dry mixture then pour in the wet mixture.
6. Mix thoroughly until a smooth batter is achieved. But be careful not to over mix it.
7. Spoon the donut batter evenly into each well of the donut pan; filling ¾ full.
8. Bake for 10 minutes or until donuts spring back when softly touched.
9. Cool donuts in the pan for 5 minutes before transferring them to a wire rack.
10. Spread the frosting glaze on the cooled donuts.
11. Place back on the rack.
12. While glaze is still wet, sprinkle with valentine's sprinkles

To make the frosting

1. Beat together all of the glaze ingredients until it becomes light and fluffy.

Creamy Christmas Donut

Feel the holidays with this cream cheese topped glazed baked donuts. You can feel the Christmas spirit with the festive Christmas sprinkles on top.

MAKES: 6 DONUTS
PREPARATION TIME: 10 minutes
BAKING TIME: 15 minutes

1 cup flour
6 tablespoons sugar
1 teaspoon salt
6 tablespoons skim milk
¼ teaspoon white vinegar
1 teaspoon baking powder
1 egg
½ teaspoon vanilla
¼ teaspoon cinnamon
1/8 teaspoon ground ginger
1/8 teaspoon ground nutmeg
1 tablespoon melted butter

Topping:
cream cheese

Glaze:
½ cup powder sugar
½ teaspoon vanilla
½ teaspoon butter flavor
2 teaspoon skim milk
Christmas Sprinkles

Directions

1. Preheat the oven to 325°F.
2. In a large mixer add in the dry ingredients then mix in the wet ingredients until the batter is well combined.
3. Spray a donut pan with cooking spray and then spoon in the batter.
4. Fill the pan well about ¾ full to allow a little room for the donut to rise.
5. Bake these in the oven 10 minutes or until they appear to have a nice brown color. In order to make these as gluten-free donuts, you would need to bake them for an extra 5 minutes (total 15 minutes). Use a toothpick to do the testing in the middle and check if it comes out clean. A clean toothpick means that they are done.
6. While the donuts are baking mix together the glaze ingredients adding more milk if needed.
7. Let the donuts cool on a wire rack.
8. Once the donuts have cooled drizzle the glaze over the donuts or ice with your favorite icing.
9. Top with festive Christmas sprinkles.

Skewered Snowmen

This is a really cute holiday treat for the kids. You can also have fun assembling these donuts together with the kids.

MAKES: 21 DONUT HOLES or 7 SNOWMEN
PREPARATION TIME: 30 minutes
BAKING TIME: 9 minutes

1/3 cup milk
1 teaspoon vinegar
3 tablespoons unsalted butter
½ cup white whole wheat flour
½ cup unbleached all-purpose flour
1 teaspoon baking powder, free of aluminum
¼ teaspoon sea salt
1/8 teaspoon nutmeg, fresh
¼ cup sugar
2 tablespoons honey
1 large egg
¼ vanilla bean

For the coating and decoration:
5 tablespoons unsalted butter
1/3 cup powdered sugar
1 package multi-colored gel candies
1 pack of fruit roll-ups or sour patch straws
black icing
wooden skewers
clear plastic baggies
ribbon

Directions

1. Preheat oven to 400°F.
2. In a small bowl, mix together milk and vinegar.
3. Allow to sit for about 5 minutes to curdle.
4. Melt butter in another small bowl and set aside to cool.
5. Whisk together flours, baking powder, sea salt, and nutmeg in a larger bowl; then set aside.
6. Whisk in sugar, honey, egg, and vanilla bean seeds until evenly combined into the bowl of melted butter.
7. Add in curdled milk.
8. Whisk together wet and dry ingredients until just combined without over mixing.
9. Spray a baby donut pan.
10. Evenly distribute batter in each pan well.
11. Bake for 9 minutes.
12. Allow donuts to cool for a minute before removing from pan and placing on a cooling rack to cool completely.
13. Dip each donut in butter before coating in the powdered sugar mixture.

To make the coating

1. Melt butter.
2. In a small bowl, mix together cinnamon and sugar.
3. Put powdered sugar in a separate bowl.

To assemble

1. Slide three coated donuts into a wooden skewer.
2. Cut green candies in half.
3. Place cut candies in the holes of the two bottom donuts to make buttons.
4. Place an orange candy in the hole of the top donut for the nose.
5. Gently wrap a fruit roll-up and place between the top and second donuts to make a scarf.
6. Dip a toothpick into black icing and draw dots to

form eyes and smile on the top donut.
7. Wrap each snowman individually with baggies and ribbon.

Merry Reindeer and Snowman

These baked chocolate coated mini donuts are way too cute not to try.
These are a perfect treat for the kids on the holidays.

MAKES: 24 MINI DONUTS
PREPARATION TIME: 10 minutes
BAKING TIME: 5 minutes

For the batter:
1 cup flour
½ cup low fat eggnog
scant ½ cup sugar
½ tablespoons baking powder
2 teaspoon cinnamon
½ teaspoon nutmeg
1 egg
4 teaspoon canola oil

For the decoration:
mini pretzel twists, form into antler-like pieces
coated chocolate candies in red and orange colors
¾ cup semi-sweet chocolate, melted
¾ white chocolate, melted
large white pearl sprinkles
mini chocolate chips

Directions

1. Preheat the oven to 325°F.
2. In a large mixer add in first the dry ingredients.
3. Then mix in the wet ingredients until the batter is well combined.
4. Grease a mini donut pan liberally.
5. Fill each with about 1 and ½ teaspoons of batter. Do not overfill so they won't look like cupcakes.
6. Bake for 3 to 5 minutes.
7. Cool them completely before decorating.

For the reindeer design

1. Use a pretzel to gently poke tops of each donut to create holes. Doing this allows you to locate the holes where you will insert the antlers. The chocolate that will sink to it will also act as glue for the antlers.
2. Dip the one side of the donut in the melted semi-sweet chocolate. Twist gently to remove excess and allow it to drip back into the bowl.
3. Turn right side up and insert pretzel antlers.
4. Place on a wire rack.
5. Gently drop a red candy into the donut's hole. If it sinks down too deep, drop another one.
6. Place two white pearl sprinkles above the nose to form as reindeer's eyes.

For the snowman design

1. Dip a donut into melted white chocolate the place on the rack.
2. Drop an orange candy in its hole, drop another one if needed.
3. Use mini chocolate chips to create snowman's eyes and mouth.
4. Allow the decorated donuts to sit at room temp for the chocolate to set, or chill them for faster results.

Glazed Baby Party Donuts

These bite-sized donuts are a must have for on-the-go snacking and any kid's parties. The kids will surely come asking for more.

MAKES: 5 Dozens Baby DONUTS
PREPARATION TIME: 10 minutes
BAKING TIME: 8 minutes

2/3 cup all-purpose gluten free flour
1/3 cup cocoa powder
1/3 cup granulated sugar
¼ teaspoon ground nutmeg
¼ teaspoon xanthan gum
¼ cup canola oil
¼ cup unsweetened applesauce

Vanilla glaze:
1 cup confectioner's sugar
1 tbsp. milk
½ teaspoon vanilla extract
4 drops of liquid blue food coloring
White nonpareils

Directions

1. Preheat oven to 425°F.
2. Spray mini donut pan with nonstick cooking spray.
3. In large mixing bowl, sift together all dry ingredients

except for vanilla seeds.

4. Add in buttermilk, vanilla extract, vanilla seeds, eggs, and butter and beat until just combined.
5. Fill each donut well for approximately ½ full.
6. Bake 5-8 minutes or until the top of the donut springs back when touched.
7. Let cool in pan for 5 minutes before removing and transferred on a cooling rack.

For the glaze

1. In small bowl, stir together sugar, vanilla extract, and milk until sugar is completely dissolved. Add food coloring and stir until color becomes uniform.
2. Finish donuts with vanilla glaze.

Mini Tricky Treat Donuts

Pumpkins are not just for carving a Jack o' Lantern on Halloween. They are also very nutritious to blend in these chocolate glazed donuts which are a perfect for kids treat on Halloween.

MAKES: 24 Mini DONUTS
PREPARATION TIME: 25 minutes
BAKING TIME: 12 minutes

½ cup of vegetable oil
3 large eggs
1½ cups of granulated sugar
1½ cups of canned pure pumpkin
2 teaspoons of ground cinnamon
1½ teaspoons of kosher salt
1½ teaspoons of baking powder
1¾ cup of flour, plus two tablespoons

Chocolate Glaze:
¾ cup semi-sweet chocolate chips
3 tablespoons butter
1 tablespoon light corn syrup
¼ teaspoon vanilla extract

Topping:
Halloween sprinkles

Directions

1. Preheat oven to 350°F
2. Lightly grease donut pan with butter.
3. In the bowl with a stand mixer, combine all of the ingredients except for the flour.
4. Mix until well combined and smooth.
5. Add flour and continue to stir on low speed, just until combined. Be careful not to over mix.
6. Transfer batter to a gallon sized pastry bag and snip off the tip.
7. Pipe batter into donut pan wells, filling each well about half way full.
8. Bake 10-12 minutes or until donut pushes back when touched gently.
9. Remove from the oven and let cool there for about 5 minutes then transfer donuts on a wire cooling rack.
10. Spread warm glaze over top of each donut, letting it drizzle down the sides.
11. Finish with sprinkles.

To make the glaze

1. In a double boiler over hot but not boiling water, combine chocolate chips, corn syrup, and butter. Stir well until chips are melted and mixture is smooth. Remove from heat then add vanilla.

Chocolaty Spooky Spiders Donuts

These little chocolaty crawlies has spooky looking eyes staring at you.
This chocolate covered mini donut is a creepy and delicious treat for
Halloween parties.

MAKES: 20 MINI DONUTS
PREPARATION TIME: 45 minutes
BAKING TIME: 8 minutes

---

2 cups flour
1 cup sugar
½ cup cocoa powder
½ cup mini chocolate chips
1 teaspoon baking soda
1 teaspoon vanilla extract
2 eggs
¾ sour cream
½ cup milk
½ cup vegetable oil

For the coating and decorations:
1 cup heavy cream
1 cup bittersweet chocolate
¼ package chocolate bark
1 package licorice twists
eyeball sprinkles, aluminum-free

Directions

1. Preheat oven to 375°F.
2. In a medium mixing bowl, combine all the dry ingredients, but exclude the chocolate chips.
3. In a small bowl, beat together the dry ingredients.
4. Stir the wet ingredients into the dry until just

combined.

5. Chop chocolate chips and fold into the batter.
6. Spoon in a greased donut pan.
7. Bake for 8 minutes or until the tops spring back when touched.
8. Let the donuts cool completely in the pan.
9. Dip each donut wholly into the frosting.
10. Place frosted donuts on cooling rack for frosting to set.

To make chocolate frosting

1. Heat heavy cream in a small pot. Remove from stove once it begins to boil.
2. Pour heated cream into bowl of chopped chocolate.
3. Stir and mix until chocolate is melted completely.
4. Let frosting cool for a few minutes.

To Assemble

1. Melt the chocolate in a small bowl until smooth and melted.
2. While it melts, cut the licorice into about ½" long or enough to be spider legs.
3. Dip the tip of each licorice piece into the melted chocolate and gently set it against the sides of the donut, 4 licorice pieces per side.
4. Allow the legs to set before moving the donut.
5. Attach 2 eyeballs onto each donut using some of the melted chocolate as glue.
6. Again, let set.

Happy Clown Cake Donuts

Any birthday party will surely be happy with these clown cake donuts. Your kids will definitely enjoy this colorful clown goody at a birthday party.

MAKES: 12 DONUTS
PREPARATION TIME: 15 minutes
BAKING TIME: 8 minutes

2 cups all-purpose flour, sifted
¾ cup granulated sugar
2 teaspoons baking powder
½ teaspoon salt
¾ cup buttermilk
1 teaspoon vanilla extract
2 eggs, lightly beaten
2 tablespoon butter, melted
Seeds from one vanilla bean
yellow, red, orange, green, blue, purple gel food colorings

Directions

1. Preheat oven to 425°F.
2. Spray donut pan with nonstick cooking spray.
3. In large mixing bowl, sift together all dry ingredients.
4. Add in the buttermilk, vanilla extract, vanilla seeds,

eggs, and butter and beat until just combined.

5. Divide the batter into 6 bowls.
6. Color each with red, purple, green, orange, yellow, and blue.
7. Scrape each colored batter into separate small sandwich bags.
8. Put each bag into a small glass for support.
9. Cut a small hole from the corner of the yellow bag and press gently to place a big dot of batter into each pan well, half way full.
10. Do the same with all the colors. Estimate piping of each color to make sure there's enough space for all.
11. Bake for 4-8 minutes or until the tops of donuts spring back when pressed.
12. Let cool in pan for 5 minutes before removing them.

Love Donuts with Dark Chocolate Ganache

Surprise everyone you love this Valentine's Day with these baked love donuts delicately treated with dark chocolate ganache. This is a perfect way to start or finish a special love day.

MAKES: 6 DONUTS
PREPARATION TIME: 25 minutes
BAKING TIME: 15 minutes

½ cup vanilla almond milk
½ teaspoon lemon juice
½ teaspoon vanilla extract
½ teaspoon coffee extract
1 tablespoon agave nectar
1/8 cup light brown sugar
1 cup whole wheat pastry flour
1/8 cup cocoa powder
¼ teaspoon salt
¼ teaspoon baking powder
¼ teaspoon baking soda
1/8 cup vegan chocolate chips, crushed using a food processor

For the Ganache:
½ cup vegan chocolate chips
3 tablespoons vanilla almond milk, heated
Heart-shaped nonpareils for top

Directions

1. Preheat oven to 350°F.
2. Spray a heart-shaped donut pan lightly with oil and set aside.
3. Whisk together wet ingredients including brown sugar until it's foamy.

4. Combine remaining ingredients in a large bowl.
5. Then add the wet mixture and fold in.
6. Spoon batter into donut pan, filling each donut well to the top.
7. Bake 15 minutes or until a toothpick comes out clean.
8. While baking, prepare the ganache.
9. Remove from oven and let cool there for few minutes.
10. When donuts are cool enough to handle, dip one side in the prepared ganache.
11. Place them on a cooling rack.
12. Sprinkle some heart nonpareils.

To make the ganache

1. Melt chocolate in the microwave or in a double boiler.
2. Add heated almond milk 1 teaspoon at a time, stirring briskly to combine until you reach the right consistency. It should be thicker than a sauce.
3. Continue to reheat and melt chocolate as you add in liquid.

Confetti Donuts

These fluffy baked vanilla glazed donuts are a fun twist to the regular confetti cake. These are a perfect birthday treat for children's birthday parties.

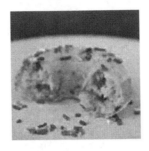

MAKES: 6 DONUTS
PREPARATION TIME: 10 minutes
BAKING TIME: 15 minutes

¼ cup all-purpose flour
1 tablespoon granulated sugar
1 teaspoon baking powder
1/8 teaspoon salt
1/3 cup milk
1 large egg
2 tablespoons honey
1½ tablespoons plain Greek yogurt
½ teaspoon vanilla extract
¼ teaspoon almond extract
1½ tablespoons jimmies

For the vanilla glaze:
½ cup sifted confectioners' sugar,
1 tablespoon softened butter
¼ teaspoon vanilla extract
1/8 teaspoon salt
1 tablespoon milk
More jimmies for top

Directions

1. Preheat the oven to 350°F.
2. Whisk together the dry ingredients in a medium-sized mixing bowl.
3. In a separate bowl, beat the wet ingredients together until foamy.
4. Pour the liquid mixture all at once into the dry mixture and stir just until combined.
5. Then add the jimmies and stir until they are evenly distributed.
6. Grease the donut pan.
7. Fill each well to half full.
8. Bake the donuts in the preheated for 13 to 15 minutes or till donuts will spring back when touched gently, and have started to brown on top.
9. Remove the donuts from the oven and let cool there for a few minutes.
10. Remove them carefully from the pan using a spatula then to a wire rack.
11. By the time donuts have cooled slightly, dip the tops of each in the glaze, and then return it to the wire rack to finish cooling and to allow glaze to set.
12. Sprinkle additional jimmies.

To make the vanilla glaze

1. Combine all glaze ingredients in a small bowl. Stir until the glaze turns smooth and well blended.

Independence Day Donut Holes Cake

*Celebrate freedom with this frosted baked chocolate cake donut holes.
You can probably have the entire family assist in assembling this
Independence Day donut holes cake.*

MAKES: 60 DONUTS
PREPARATION TIME: 1 hour plus

---

*60 pieces already baked chocolate cake donut holes
2 cans (16 ounces each) white frosting, melted and then divided
red concentrated paste food coloring
¾ teaspoon royal blue concentrated paste food coloring
2 teaspoon white nonpareils and/or star-shaped sprinkles*

Directions

1. In bowl, combine 1 can of melted frosting and enough red food coloring (about 3/4 teaspoon) to create desired red shade.
2. One at a time, dip 48 donut holes in red frosting to coat, arrange on wire rack set on cookie sheet.
3. Set aside 1/3 cup white frosting.
4. In a bowl, mix remaining white frosting and enough blue food coloring (about ¾ teaspoon) to create preferred shade of blue.
5. Dip remaining 12 donut balls in blue frosting, place on wire rack and sprinkle with white nonpareils and stars.
6. Drizzle reserved white frosting over red holes.
7. Chill for an hour or until set.

To assemble

1. On a platter, arrange 3 blue donut holes, then 3 red

donuts in a vertical line.

2. Repeat 3 times to create 4 blue-and-red rows.
3. Add remaining red donuts for a total of 6 rows of all red donut pops.
4. Chill.
5. Serve with lollipop sticks on the side.

July 4th Marshmallow Wacko

Be free with these marshmallow frosted baked wacko donuts. This is so fun and easy to assemble and your whole family will love them.

MAKES: 12 DONUTS
PREPARATION TIME: 30 minutes
BAKING TIME: 7 minutes

---

2 cups cake flour, sifted
¾ cup granulated sugar
2 teaspoons baking powder
¼ teaspoon ground nutmeg
1 teaspoon kosher salt
¾ cup buttermilk
2 eggs
2 tablespoons butter, melted

For the marshmallow frosting:
2 egg whites
¼ teaspoon salt
¼ cup granulated sugar
¾ cup corn syrup
1 teaspoon vanilla extract
red food coloring
blue food coloring

Directions

1. Preheat oven to 425°F.
2. Spray donut pan with nonstick cooking spray.
3. In large mixing bowl, mix together flour, nutmeg, sugar, baking powder, and salt.
4. Add buttermilk, eggs and butter.
5. Beat until just combined.
6. Fill each donut cup approximately 2/3 full.

To make the marshmallow frosting

1. In a stand mixer with a whisk attachment, beat egg whites and salt until it becomes frothy.
2. Gradually add in sugar, beating until soft peaks form.
3. Heat syrup in a glass microwaveable dish until it boils.
4. Pour syrup in thin stream over egg white mixture, in small amounts at a time. Beating on high speed until harder peaks form.
5. Add vanilla and beat until glossy.
6. Divide the frosting in three bowls.
7. Make the two blue and red.

To assemble

1. Spread the white frosting all over the cooled donut.
2. Add the red frosting to a piping bag and make three lines across the donut.
3. Place the donut in the fridge for a few minutes to allow the frosting to set.
4. After a few minutes take the donuts out, add the blue frosting to another piping bag and make blue dots on them wherever you desire.
5. Once done, return the donuts back in the fridge to let the blue frosting set before serving.

Easter 'Coco-nest' Donuts

Have fun preparing and assembling these Easter donuts with your kids. They will surely love these fluffy donuts topped with coconut and colored candy to fit an Easter party.

MAKES: 12 DONUTS
PREPARATION TIME: 25 minutes
BAKING TIME: 15 minutes

---

1 cup all-purpose flour
1 teaspoon baking powder
¼ teaspoon baking soda
½ teaspoon salt
1/3 cup granulated sugar
2 tablespoons cold butter
¼ cup scalded milk
¼ cup plain yogurt
1 beaten egg

For the decorations:
1 cup confectioner's sugar
½ tablespoon boiling water, extra if needed
almond extract
½ cup shredded coconuts
Green liquid food dye
tiny colorful egg-shaped candies

Directions

1. Preheat the oven to 350°F.
2. In a large bowl, mix together the dry ingredients.
3. Melt the butter.
4. Pour in the egg, yogurt and milk, and melted butter into the dry mixture, and then stir to combine. Be careful not to over-mix.
5. Pipe batter into a greased donut pan to half way full in each well.
6. Bake for 15 minutes or until springy.
7. Allow to cool in the pan for a few minutes then transfer donuts on a cooling rack.

To make the decorations

1. Put confectioner's sugar in a bowl and pour in a tiny bit of boiling water.
2. Whisk until smooth and pretty runny. (If it is too thick, gradually add very little amounts of water; if it's too thin, add just a little bit of sugar.)
3. Add 2 or 3 drops almond extract.
4. Add few drops of food dye. Gradually until you reach desired greenness of coconut which will serve as grass.
5. In a bowl, dye shredded coconut with green. Few drops will do.

To assemble

1. Dip each cooled donut half way into the green glaze.
2. Tap any excess glaze back to the bowl.
3. Then dip the glazed donut into the colored coconut.
4. Place it back on the rack.
5. Place some candies in the donut hole.

Easter Bunny Powdered Donut Holes

Easter bunny donut holes are fun-filled sweet donuts that are perfect for Easter. These are covered with powdered sugar and decorated with lots of stuff like sprinkles, mallows, jelly beans, and more.

MAKES: 36 DONUT HOLES
PREPARATION TIME: 40 minutes
BAKING TIME: 20 minutes

---

8 tablespoons unsalted butter that is warmed at room temperature
4 tablespoons low-fat plain yogurt
¾ cup plus 2 tablespoons sugar
2 large eggs
3 cups all-purpose flour
½ tablespoons plus 1 teaspoon baking powder
¼ teaspoon baking soda
¾ plus 1/8 teaspoon salt
½ teaspoon ground nutmeg
½ cup plus 1/3 cup milk
2 tablespoons cup buttermilk
Canola oil cooking spray
1 cup powdered sugar, and some extra - enough to cover the whole donuts

For Decoration:
72 candy eyes balls
36 marshmallows
pink sprinkles
store bought black icing

store bought white frosting
18 pink jelly beans, cut in half
toothpicks

Directions

1. Place a rack in the middle of the oven and preheat oven to 350°F.
2. In a large bowl, cream the butter and sugar.
3. Beat in the eggs one at a time until just mixed in.
4. In a medium bowl, sift together all remaining dry ingredients.
5. In another small bowl, combine the milk and buttermilk.
6. With a wooden spoon, mix ¼ of the dry ingredients into the butter mixture.
7. Then mix in 1/3 of the milk mixture.
8. Keep on mixing in the remaining dry and wet ingredients alternately, always ending with the dry. Mix until well combined and smooth, but not to over mix.
9. Grease donut-hole/mini muffin pan.
10. Scoop enough batter into each well until batter evens out to the rim.
11. Bake until firm to the touch, for about 18-20 minutes.
12. When the donuts are cool enough to handle, working in batches, spray a few of the donut holes with cooking spray.
13. Roll in powdered sugar. Make sure to coat the donuts thickly.
14. Continue with remaining donut holes.

Assemble the Bunny Head

1. Slice the two ends off the marshmallows, making about 1/3 on an inch pieces.

2. Sprinkle the pink sprinkles over the cut side of the marshmallows.
3. Carefully pinch together marshmallows to form an oval shape like bunny ears.
4. Stick toothpick in the bottom of the era-shaped marshmallow and secure into the top of the donut hole.
5. Repeat with the second ear.
6. Using the white frosting as glue, fasten the eyes and halved jelly bean noses to the face.
7. Use the black icing to make whiskers.

Mother's Day Special Baked Lite Donut

Mother's day is the perfect special time to treat your mom with these baked lite strawberry flavored donuts. Mother's will surely have a relaxing time enjoying these goodies.

MAKES: 6 DONUTS
PREPARATION TIME: 10 minutes
BAKING TIME: 15 minutes

¾ cup gluten-free flour
¼ cup coconut sugar
½ teaspoon baking powder
¼ teaspoon baking soda
1/8 teaspoon salt
1 egg
½ of a 6-ounce container strawberry Greek yogurt
3 tablespoons canola oil
3 tablespoons buttermilk

For the glaze:
1/5 cup pureed fresh strawberries
½ cup powdered sugar

Directions

1. Preheat oven to 325°F.

2. Spray donut pan with non-stick baking spray.
3. In a large mixing bowl, sift together all dry ingredients.
4. In medium-sized bowl, whisk together all wet ingredients.
5. Gradually pour wet ingredients to the dry ingredients mixture while combining well until the entire batter is combined.
6. Using a pastry bag, pipe batter into donut pan filling while each well up to ¾ full.
7. Bake for 15 minutes until a tester inserted into the center of the donut comes out clean.
8. Cool donuts in the pan before transferring on wire baking rack.
9. While donuts are cooling, prepare glaze.
10. Drizzle glaze over cooled donuts, or dip each into the glaze to coat wholly.

To make the glaze

1. Whisk together the strawberry puree and powdered sugar to combine.